Rebirth of Pragmatism (The Book on Fun)

Ray Santoli

ISBN 978-1-304-18746-8

Rebirth of Pragmatism (The Book on Fun)

Contents

Preface

With all due respect to the collective mindsets of modern-day readers, I suspect that the vast majority of our collective minds aren't of the general constitution to allow us to comprehend complex concepts; at least not, perhaps, to the extent to which our forefathers were once able. I arrived at this conclusion as a result of having been exposed, at various times over the years, to various written excerpts from some of the leading minds of science of the late nineteenth century. And upon having done so, found myself rather poorly equipped to directly follow some of the paths of their reasoning. If this is indeed the case that we, as a society, aren't quite as erudite as we once were, then I'm sure that there are any number of theories that could possibly provide explanations as to the root cause of this, our "dumbing down," that's possibly occurred. But any conclusions that might be drawn from any such theories would likely be, for whatever reason, of little interest to me. My interest in this dumbing down of our society serves a strictly selfish and professional one, as I'm hoping that my general lack of acumen in *discussing* complex concepts will coincide nicely with what I propose to be the general population's general lack of ability in *comprehending* them; which, should it turn out to actually be the case, might thereby render this work to be an enjoyable, agreeable source of entertainment and/or education for the vast majority of potential readers out there.

In the presentation of this material, I'll be making several assumptions about you, the reader: (1) that you have a lot of "down time"; (2) that you don't mind reading a good book; and (3) that you currently don't have anything else good to read. If this is indeed the case, then I'm hoping that you'll cut me some slack in case this *doesn't* happen to be the enjoyable, agreeable read that I've intended for it to be for you, because I'm at least *trying* to contribute to your entertainment or education. With that deferential suggestion either aside if you enjoy the book or in mind if you don't, it occurs to me that the phrase "This is some good shit" is the greatest thing that a reader can say about a book. I'd consider it the ultimate compliment if you, as the reader, were to come to that spontaneous conclusion at some point during your read. In fact, in my opinion, anyone who *doesn't,* at some point, come to that spontaneous conclusion about *any* book that he or she is reading should be allowed to go back and get a refund on that book, because that book isn't worth the paper that it's printed on. But it's been my observation that as long as the content is well-constructed and well-organized, as far as the minds of readers are concerned, if the actual ideas or concepts that are presented within the book itself are ill-conceived, it's of secondary importance to the reader's enjoyment. But, let's of course hope that that sentiment doesn't apply here. Enjoy!

Pragmatic Writing

I'll be bearing parts of my soul on these pages, as the following insights will have originated from the heart. And when the expressed thoughts come from deep inside, it's almost as if the words write themselves. I suspect that's the reason why the books that I write never take that long for me to finish (that, plus they're short). Aside from the gratification that an author receives from making book sales and getting his or her opinions on the record, he or she learns more about him or herself by means of the writing process. Writing reveals who the writer is. To comprehend my writing is to see the world through my eyes and to know who I am. It's a path of discovery. The end product is already inside of the writer before he or she begins. It simply has to be refined out.

Also, aside from the author's knowledge and application of the correct words and phrases that are required to accurately express his or her thoughts, the most important tool that he or she possesses is the ability to reread his or her material with fresh, new eyes every day—in other words, his or her ability to actively engage in the editing process. I feel that practically anyone who chooses to engage in this "contemplation followed by editing" process can become capable of unveiling the revelations that writing can provide for oneself. Intelligent or experienced people can discover new insights about the world and the human experience that could dwarf anything that I could ever figure out. This particular effort of mine is hopefully a contribution to that self-same cause, for whatever it's worth. It will be a philosophical endeavor, as philosophy is a search for truth.

Some of the thoughts that will be expressed here will perhaps seem to be obvious observations to some readers, and such thoughts, therefore, might not seem to be worth mentioning to them. But I'm afraid that such thoughts are all that I have to offer. Some of these thoughts may end up being considered by some (if not all) of you to be total hogwash, as I may be flat-out mistaken in some of the views and assumptions that I'll be respectively taking and making. Where the truth lies, I leave to the surmise of the reader. Also, perhaps, unbeknownst to me, any of whatever portion of this material which may turn out to be of any actual sentimental validity on my own part may turn out to have already been expressed by various other writers at various other times throughout the course of history. But whatever the case may be, this offering will end up revealing myself to be, literally, an open book. However pedestrian, or absurd, or hopefully, *enlightened*, my thoughts may either prove or prove not to be, whenever it's all said and done, these thoughts will have resulted in myself having produced a clearer perspective of who I am. And, if it turns out that it *has* all been said before, well then, these will simply just have to be *My Favorite Sentiments of Western Civilization*. But if it turns out that I'm *not* simply repeating others' convictions and sentiments, and that I *am* essentially correct in some of my suppositions, I'll still have to acknowledge the fact that there are always exceptions to the rule—people for whom conventional wisdom doesn't apply. And in the end, whether those exceptions end up applying to myself or yourself in regard to what's being written here, I'm hoping that you'll bear that stipulation in mind as we embark on this journey together.

A person is his beliefs. To know what you believe in is to know who you are. This writing process will hopefully enable me to extract some of my beliefs from my soul. We don't know or understand our own souls. We either occasionally have minor moments of inspired revelation about who we are, or as I believe is more often the case, we read or hear about other beliefs that other people currently hold or have held and we bounce them off our own souls to see if they resonate. As far as I know, these are the only two methods by which people grow to understand their own natures. It seems that my own nature leans more towards the pragmatic side of the "sensibilities spectrum," as thoughts relating to the application of knowledge seem to resonate the loudest with me. Knowledge without utility is trivia. Trivia is by definition useless. Why bother with useless information?

There's a lot of information available to be read out there in the world, but how much of it is useful? I can't tell you how many times I've suffered through reading a book in hopes of gleaning something worthwhile from it that I might later use towards an increase in my own quality of life, only to wind up having reached the end of it having been left "none the wiser" for the experience. I'm making a concerted effort here to provide only useful information for the reader. Instead of writing, as some authors have done (and to great sales success I might add), about topics such as the weaknesses in our minds that are likely preventing us from anticipating what will make us happy in life, or the weaknesses in our brains that are likely preventing us from making good decisions in life, I suggested to myself that it might be more worthwhile to direct my efforts towards figuring out what would actually *make* us all happy and what would actually *be* some good decisions for us to make.

But this type of self-revealing writing that I'm talking about can also serve an additional pragmatic purpose in the author/reader relationship besides the one that's designed around the simple transmission and absorption of the reading material itself. For, if the author's sentiments are genuine, then this type of "window into his or her soul" (if also used in conjunction with whatever references and public records are available concerning the author) can provide potential acquaintances or employers of the author with insightful information regarding the general values and principles that he or she holds and can even provide, perhaps, a general overview into his or her mentality. And the information that can be gleaned from such disclosure could then be used by said potential acquaintances or employers to aid them in their respective decision-making processes as to whether or not the author should be deemed worthy of becoming a future acquaintance or employee of theirs, whichever the case may be. This type of voluntary disclosure on the part of prospective employees I think would be, at the least, a much more preferable alternative than the current practice of employers asking job applicants about their criminal records. Because due to the fact that "ex-cons" have paid their debt to society, it seems that asking any prospective employees about their criminal record/past should be considered an unconstitutional act on the parts of employers. But I digress.

When potential acquaintances or employers meet a person, that person is at first an unknown commodity to them. Couldn't everyone benefit from having at their disposal a potential reference tool such as the one that I'm providing here (and ostensibly proposing that others provide about themselves, as well) to use in their respective decision-making processes as to whether to accept or reject whichever person they're currently considering to become either a future acquaintance or employee of theirs? I believe *I* certainly would benefit from having such a tool at *my* disposal in order to help me make quicker, more accurate determination in regards to others' character. Now that I think of it, *everyone* should provide information about themselves such that I'm providing here about myself. Due to the fact that the type of subject matter that I'm covering here is of such a personal and revealing nature, the information that would be contained in such a document could provide an almost immediate and clear picture of who a person is, instead of the usual, drawn out process that's normally required by us to find out what values and principles a person truly represents. But it also has to be mentioned and understood, of course, that such a system of disclosure could only be as accurate as its providers were to be honest.

Should this form of disclosure ever actually become popularized, anyone who might be having trouble figuring out what to right about him or herself could use this book's format as a template, using the broad topics that are represented here in the different chapters as a primer and then making his or her own belief-based statements regarding each one. And furthermore, people could also use what I've specifically written in regard to each topic as a potential barometer for determining the degree to which they might be willing to disclose information about themselves. People could either provide their own beliefs regarding a topic or they could simply import any famous quotations with which they sympathize to help them express their own views regarding that topic. Also, there's plenty more that can be said in regard to each of the subject areas that I've chosen, and there are plenty of other subject areas that can be discussed, as well. Of course, any views that a person might feel might be of too personal or provocative a nature to be released for public scrutiny could simply be neglected to be mentioned by him or her. Look at the trend that's already been established in our society. People want the world to know who they are. First, there was *myspace.com*, the first popular social network website, in which people were only capable of sharing a rather shallow side of themselves to others. Then there was *facebook.com*, which is currently the most popular social network website, which is likely a direct result of its increased capability for its members to reveal personal information about themselves. Now, personal insight can be taken to the next level with something like I've presented here; perhaps calling it something like, "*beliefbook.com*: a social network website that's dedicated to providing its users with a friendly form of investigation into both their own and anyone else's life who's willing to share."

Pragmatic Philosophy

I think it would only be natural for someone to assume that an American school of thought that entitled itself "Pragmatism" would focus itself on the useful application of ideas, since that's, of course, the literal definition of the word. But one would be mistaken in that assumption if one were to happen to make it, due to the presence of the turn of the nineteenth century philosophical movement that went under that same name, but which didn't make the useful application of ideas its primary focus at all. Instead, like the other philosophical movements of its day, its founders made seemingly arbitrary political, social, and economic tenets the focus of its collective cause (if anyone's interested in further investigation into their school of thought, the founders of Pragmatism are generally considered to be William James, Charles Peirce, and John Dewey, as I understand it). My mentioning of their movement isn't done to discredit any of the contributions or advancements to modern thought that their so-called form of Pragmatism may have achieved, but instead, to delineate my intentions as far as the use of the word is concerned; and to also disassociate myself from their philosophical beliefs. It's also done in order to dare not suggest that any of my own comments or suggestions might deserve any equal consideration or credit with any of theirs, as I openly admit that any one of them could easily have thought "circles" around me (but I *would* love to wear those huge mutton-chop sideburns that they wore. I hope those come back into style someday, because that's my favorite type of facial hair.). Although I consider myself a pragmatist in the *literal* sense, I don't consider myself one in the *pure* sense, as it seems to me that a pure form of pragmatism might necessarily or naturally involve a presumption or predisposition towards an amoral, or "ends justifying the means," approach to problem-solving. But since morality is perhaps the single-most defining characteristic of humanity, I could only in good conscience be in support of the practice of a morally-based form of pragmatism. If I could, I'd like to reclaim the term "Pragmatism" back from those nineteenth and twentieth century philosophers, whom I believe performed a disservice to the word by attaching it to their actually "nonpragmatic" philosophies.

With those potential sources of confusion hopefully dispelled, I'll begin my pragmatic inquiry into this world. What is of the utmost or ultimate importance in life? The secular response to this question would likely be "happiness." Our country's Declaration of Independence espouses as much with its extolling of our citizenry's "pursuit of" it. Happiness can be defined in terms of quality of life. All actions and goals in life should generally be geared toward this end whenever it's appropriate and/or convenience allows. And I believe that anything that results in a person receiving an increase in his or her quality of life can be considered useful. I also, therefore, believe that the value of any given thought or activity can be determined by considering its relative usefulness or utility.

9

But a potential problem exists when considering happiness in this context. Did you notice my use of the word "secular" in my response to the question of "What's important in life?" There's a potentially important aspect to this discussion that I feel needs to be addressed. It has to do with the concerns of the secular vs. the concerns of the spiritual. The question is this: should secular concerns in life be worth considering at all? The New Testament states that "He who finds his life shall lose it, and he who loses his life shall find it." But what does "finding your life" and "losing your life" entail in this Biblical context? I suggest that "finding your life" in the Biblical context means satisfying the desires of your "genetic man," and by contrast, that "losing your life" in this context means willfully subjugating the desires of your "genetic man" in deference towards satisfying the obligations of your "spiritual man." And "pursuing happiness" is perhaps a strictly genetic desire. Said Bible verse, then, implies that secular concerns should be considered irrelevant to us in our daily lives. So, if one were to use the New Testament as a guideline for determining what should be important for one's own self in life, the conclusion that all humans might be expected to draw might be words to the effect that, "We should all mortify our desires of the flesh in deference towards the concerns of the afterlife, which are spiritual in nature." And I don't doubt that such an approach to life would be the correct one for all of us to take. My problem is this: I *know* myself, and I know that I'm going to keep on trying to find happiness in life, whether it's the right thing to do or not. I'm a person who follows his own instincts, and my instincts tell me to "find happiness." The only question for me is to what lengths I'm willing to go in order to try to achieve that happiness. At any rate, "happiness pursuit" is going to continue to be a main theme in this text, whether it's a "spiritually kosher" topic to broach or not.

But although I feel like the achievement of an emotionally and physically pain-free existence is unequivocally idealized by most of us, the contemplation, or perhaps let's call it the "thoughtful revelation" (the process by which I'm attempting to figure out the methodological mistakes that I might be making in relating to this world, and also the process by which I'll be hopefully coming up with some potential solutions to any such purported mistakes) thereof, isn't necessarily the means by which a pain-free existence is procured. Knowledge isn't bliss. Ignorance is. Generally, all that a person ever accomplishes by figuring out the cause of his or her own misery is to transform him or herself from a person who was once *confused* about why he or she was so miserable into becoming a person who now *understands* why he or she's so miserable. But I feel that it's still a worthwhile process to engage in, though. Problems have to be identified before they can be solved. We just have to acknowledge the possibility that even if we find the answers to all of our questions, we may still end up living lives of dissatisfaction, and that there might end up being nothing that we can ever do about it.

A lot of cogent statements regarding our own existences have been made up until this point in the twenty-first century, but I doubt that *all* of the possible

11

ones have been made yet. I'll hopefully be providing some contributions towards that end here; comments that will hopefully be useful, and therefore, worthwhile. I'll freely admit that my comments and observations are going to lack a depth of research, though. And without research, my conclusions will therefore only amount to suspicions (and in some cases, probably *weak* suspicions). I'll venture to say that my observations are going to be similar in depth to the observations of a comedian. But I'll also hazard to say that there's no inherent shame in that. Comedians are our modern-day philosophers because they also attempt to expose truths. Truth expands knowledge. Knowledge expansion is artistic/beautiful. Therefore, truth is art/beauty. So, for this reason, comedy is a worthwhile pursuit, in and of itself. Beautifully constructed and executed art, in all of its forms, is the same. But I consider comedy to operate on a higher plateau than probably all other forms of art. In fact, I think that comedy is such a beautiful art form that I believe that the greatest country on Earth is whichever country's collective citizenry and culture is able to produce the greatest overall sense of humor within itself (not to suggest that such a delineation could ever actually be made, though). I'm a big fan of the American sense of humor, but I don't know if I can look at it objectively since I'm American. The Vietnamese people that I've met have all had a great sense of humor. There have been a ton of funny Jewish writers and performers. And aside from their wit, I suspect that New York City has been able to cement its standing as basically the capital of the business/commerce world due in large part to the overall intelligence of its Jewish population. And I also suspect that Hollywood is an entertainment and wealth capital of the world due in large part to the self-same reason. In addition to being possibly the most intelligent ethnicity, I also suspect that they're the overall funniest. Have you ever seen a comedy television program that didn't have Jewish writers? They're generally terrible.

Comedians are "people persons"; which means that they're interested in making a positive emotional connection with other people. And jokes serve them as a means towards that end. The presence of "people persons" in any interactive setting, be it the workplace, socially, or otherwise, always has the effect of providing a boost in morale for whatever individuals are present in that setting. I'm confident that it's in our society's best interest to gear our youth towards becoming ever more and more a society of "people persons."

It seems that America has a built-in cultural advantage over other nations in regard to its citizenry, and that this advantage could only seemingly grow larger and larger over time. The advantage has to do with the economic nature of our society. The opportunities for financial success that America offers its population still seem to be making it a rather magnetic destination for ambitious individuals from around the world to migrate to. Generally speaking, only financially successful or highly motivated individuals have the wherewithal to uproot themselves (and perhaps also their families) and relocate to another country. And any such individuals doing so would necessarily be in possession of a modicum of intelligence. So as long as America can continue to attract a portion of the world's intellectually elite to its shores, then it should continue to flourish, while, unfortunately, those countries that continue to lose their "best and brightest" to America will seemingly begin to languish more and more.

On the subject of cultural pride, patriotism is a natural feeling. There's no need to cultivate it. People have a natural affinity for their homelands. Flags are for people who've forgotten what country they're living in. And anyone who emphasizes the notion of patriotism has self-serving interests sustaining that sentiment. The notion of segregating teams by their nationality and consequently playing that person or team's national anthem after they've won a sporting event (i.e. the Olympics) is inherently divisive. The inhabitants of this planet would get along with each other much better if our differences were *de*-emphasized rather than celebrated.

On the subject of ulterior motives, you should neither trust anyone who smiles at you while they're telling you "facts," nor anyone who says that you "deserve" something. Smiling is used as a persuasive tool when the facts either don't add up or are useless. Generally speaking, nobody deserves anything good (except perhaps your mother because of her unconditional love for you). People who are intent on giving something to the deserving also have self-serving interests at heart.

Generally speaking, how could any of us take any pride in any of our intelligences or self-worth when none of us have ever contributed or accomplished anything of real value towards or for our society at any point in any of our lives? I suspect that the answer to this question lies in our collective feelings of self-absorption. We seem to be the most content when we're either talking about ourselves or when we ourselves are the subject of support amongst other people's conversations. And I'm no exception. I probably wish that I were some kind of celebrity just like everyone else probably wishes they were, too. But for any of us to wantonly and willingly force others to become an audience to any such demonstrations of our own personal neuroses is both a form of hijacking and of noise pollution. But at least if this presumed fact regarding our presumed feelings of self-absorption were to become circulated around enough, though, everyone might start refraining from volunteering their own self-related thoughts and comments to everyone else, because they would now realize that no one else is interested in hearing them. The cause of the disease wouldn't end up being cured this way, but it at least might become a way for the symptoms to become reduced.

By my own informal calculations, in reference to the sane portion of the American population, personal insecurity seems to be the motivating factor behind a majority of the comments that emanate from our mouths. We often only make comments so that other people will think that we're a worthwhile human being. And we also perhaps believe that if we say something of value to somebody else, then maybe our own lives aren't really as much of a waste of space and time as our consciences have likely been telling us that we should suspect that they are ... whatever helps us sleep at night, right? What I think is the greatest quote from Eastern philosophy is, "He who knows, doesn't need to say anything. And he who doesn't know, doesn't need to say anything." But although some of us might not actually have anything of real value to offer or add to any of the lives of our fellow man, as a courtesy to one another, and in recognition of the fragility of the human ego, and also in recognition of the power of depression, the arguably most important act that any one of us can perform for one another (because it's perhaps the most important part of being human itself, and it's really the least that any one of us can do for one another) is to make sure that everyone of us feels as if we're a worthwhile human being. It doesn't take much effort on any of our parts to do so, and whenever one of us succeeds in an attempt to make someone else feel better about him or herself, the effect is always potent in its boosting of that person's morale.

I also suspect that our own personal insecurities are at the root of most of the dishonest comments that emanate from our collective mouths. As admittedly distasteful as the act of lying is to most of us, it's still more preferable to many of us than providing others with information that might cast ourselves into a less than flattering light. Something that could remove all of this insecurity might be if everyone were to become subject to "world rankings" of their performances, like pro athletes who are involved in individual sports are. If this were ever to become the case in everyone's job, then no one would ever have to bother trying to "get over" on anyone else because everyone's world ranking in whatever job they were performing would be right there for everyone else to see, no matter what anyone ever happened to say regarding their own or someone else's job performance. "World rankings" are an example of a clear representation of reality versus people's *perception* of reality. The same concept would be employed if it were ever to become the case that guys had to have their "net worth" printed on their clothing. That would deter a lot of the B.S.ing that men do.

We live in a "culture of excuses," which is also a manifestation of this self-same insecurity. Imagine the widespread edification that should occur if our society would cease with its compulsion to provide explanations one to another whenever we happened to "trespass" against one another; or the widespread edification that should occur if our society would cease with its compulsion to share its troubles with one another. Unless you think that voicing your complaint will lead to a solution, keep it to yourself, because everyone else already has problems of their own to worry about. Any human society is capable of producing for itself any type of society that it so chooses. All that's required for the job is to produce a curriculum that's well-conceived and well-executed by its teachers; of which, the successive generation of learners would feel intrinsically motivated to accept, their souls being naturally capable of discerning the curriculum's worth. One justifiably emphasizable goal that I think should be present in any forward-thinking society is to eliminate the presence of yelling and violence between and among its adult population. It might not be as plausible a goal to set for ourselves regarding our child population due to their lack of emotional development, but by the time that they become adults, if they were to have been conditioned their whole lives to eliminate yelling and fighting from being such primary "go to" moves in their collective reactionary arsenals, then I believe such an initiative could easily come to meet with success.

Now, I'm not talking about split-personalities when I say that we all have voices in our heads telling us what we should or shouldn't do in life. The question is this: which voices should we listen to? I've already mentioned a potential difference that may exist between an individual's desires as related to his or her genetic makeup and his or her desires which might be an expression of his or her spirit or soul (which would operate independently of gene expression, should such a condition even exist at all). I'll now delve deeper into this question of whether or not this difference in "desire expression" actually exists. I'm going to present two schools of thought regarding the potential interplay between our souls and our emotions. The first one suggests that all of our emotional responses are messages that resound from our soul, and that both listening to and trying to enhance these so-called "visceral" responses is a worthwhile pursuit, as seeking to uncover the desires of the soul is a journey towards the divine. The second school of thought suggests that the emotional responses that relate to our *moral* decisions in life are the *only* messages that resound from our soul, and that we should, therefore, refrain from allowing any of the other emotional input that our brains happen to receive from any of these "other voices" that we have inside of us from influencing or controlling our behavior-related decisions in life.

In reference to the first school of thought regarding the potential interplay between our souls and our emotions (again, which suggests that all of our emotional responses are messages that resound from the soul), our individual souls, instincts, consciences, and emotions speak to us through our viscera; more commonly designated as our "heart" and "guts." Our intelligence, experience, and education all together constitute the voice that emanates strictly from our brain. Whenever our viscera expresses a preference either for or against our bodies taking some form of action, the brain measures the strength of that response, and then determines how much credence to lend towards the possible response options—to either go with the visceral response or not. Our souls tell us things that we could never find or figure out with our own brains. Like telling us to "believe in God" whenever our lives are in jeopardy, which, apparently, is the phenomenon that commonly takes place for soldiers on the battlefield; or "kill yourself" whenever life isn't worth living, which, apparently, is the phenomenon that commonly occurs for individuals who are so overwhelmed with negative emotion that they eventually arrive at such a conclusion. I would suspect that upon being interviewed, and upon retrospective reflection on their parts, we'd find that individuals who've failed at their individual suicide attempts would more often than not state that they believe it was the right decision for each of them to make at the time. Emotions can make a person do anything if they're strong enough.

To continue in this vein, as I believe was a thought that was first officially attributed to the mind of Aristotle, our souls are the part of us that doesn't change; our consciences are immutable. And he reasoned that that immutability was the defining characteristic of immortality; that only if something were unchanging could it become immortal. So, by use of the transitive property of logic, he thereby reasoned that our souls were immortal. Now, I'll take it a step further. If our souls are understood to be going to be making some sort of transition towards an afterlife, then what, exactly, might that transition entail? What might our souls be transitioning towards? Let's assume that the possibility of a heavenlike existence is potentially awaiting our souls; if that's the case, then by definition, that heavenly atmosphere (towards which I assume at least *some* people will be transitioning) would necessarily have to be divine in nature. And I furthermore speculate that one could come to no other reasonable conclusion than to believe that our souls would naturally be designed to experience contentment in such an environment. Although the New Testament states that our souls will take on a new appearance, or "glory," in the afterlife, our souls, though, if still being unchanged in their respective sentimentalities at that point (as could very well be the case, if, as Aristotle reasoned, immutability is one of our soul's defining characteristics), might still maintain the same desires or ambitions to which they adhered here on Earth. So, by reason of such a presumption, it could now be conjectured that what pleases our souls on Earth may very well please our souls in Heaven. And also by order of the transitive property, these presumptions must therefore lead us towards one final conclusion: that to please our souls in life is to experience the divine. And if these assumptions are true, then engaging in such a pursuit would have to be considered a worthwhile endeavor for anyone. As it may turn out, the old standard song *Heaven, I'm in Heaven* might not be that far removed from the truth.

In reference to the second school of thought regarding the potential interplay between our souls and our emotions (which, again, suggests that the emotional responses that relate to our *moral* decisions in life are the *only* messages that resound from our soul), it's a commonly held belief that our souls and consciences are synonymous with one another. And this may very well be the case. And through its distinct manner of communication with us, our consciences provide us with the emotion of "guilt" whenever we commit an immoral act. This "conscience-related" connection between our actions and our emotions is what likely prompts individuals who subscribe to the first school of thought to believe that *all* of our emotional responses in life may be connected to our souls. But this second school of thought suggests that the overwhelming majority of our emotional responses in life simply stem from the genetic makeup of our "carnal man," and that they have nothing to do with the nature of our souls, and are therefore, unworthy of any undue consideration or respect on our parts.

The answer to the question whether the root source of human emotion stems from our DNA or from our souls is likely the one that would resolve any questions regarding which of our "voices" we should be listening to. And although I'll likely never know the answer to any of these questions, I will tell you this much: that in this text, I'll be approaching the subject of the "desires of the soul" from the viewpoint of the first-mentioned school of thought (again, that postulates that *all* of our emotional responses are messages that resound from our soul), no matter how foolhardy of a decision or endeavor it may be for me to do so. And if for no other reason than for the same one that I provided as to why I'm interested in the "pursuit of happiness" in lieu of the alternative of a more spiritually-minded, "forbearance-type" of existence: because it *feels* right and I want it to *be* right. For now, I'm content to leave it to our spiritual posterity to provide us with the answers as to the root source of our emotions, and also for determining the amount of credence, if any, to lend to either of these so-called "schools of thought."

Pragmatic Lifestyle

The Victorian era writer Oscar Wilde was apparently interested in the topic of achieving fulfillment in life, as it seems to have been a major topic throughout much of his work. And, although I get the impression that posterity may perhaps be holding him in a rather contemptuous light due to his purported homosexual inclinations, and also, perhaps, for himself having led a rather indulgent lifestyle, but, based on the offerings that I've read of him, I think that he may have been in possession of qualities that may have enabled him to have become the "ideal man" as far as his attitude and approach to life were concerned. I base this judgment upon qualities that he possessed, such as his command of the English language, which revealed his intellectual prowess; the content and temperament of his discourse, which revealed both his insightful knowledge of human nature and his confident, easygoing attitude towards life; his talent for cultural criticism, which enabled him to discern the worthwhile political, social, and artistic offerings of his day and to consequently reject the worthless ones; and the quality of the seasoning of his soul, which he received from his period of incarceration (which, by the way, was implicated in his early demise), wherein he was able to mold his suffering into a tool for broadening his perspective on life. I suggest that by the end of his life, he would likely have been an ideal advisor for someone to refer to in regard to how to achieve a productive, fulfilling quality of life for one's own self. But ourselves presently being left without his guidance to aid us in this endeavor, I'm left with the proposition of simply providing my own thoughts and beliefs regarding this topic.

Quality of life can be increased through personal productivity. But what constitutes productive activity? For such a construct to be construed, productivity needs calibration. And although making money when you need it is productive, having a job doesn't necessarily confer personal productivity. Providing a person with money may be the only redeeming value that many jobs have to offer. Although practically all of the spiritually unfulfilling work that goes on in our modern society serves an ostensibly necessary role, I'm still relatively baffled by the lack of at least *vocal* resistance that our workforce provides against such "soul-disagreeing" labor. I find our world's acquiescence to our fates of "frittering our lives away" disheartening; to the extent that, despite the "self-awareness" that our particular species of animal enjoys, our lives end up being just as aimless as those of our nonhuman counterparts. It seems so much of our attention in life is focused on trivial pursuits (funny how I never noticed the irony of the game that goes by that same name, until now). But I believe it's possible to have a job that also qualifies as being personally productive, though, and it seems that's the type of work everyone should aspire to do (though I've never actually felt the dignity that "work" is purported to provide). But to learn which jobs would qualify as being productive, we first need to figure out which activities qualify as being personally productive.

I believe that game-playing, i.e. sports competition, card games, board games, casino-type gambling games, video games, etc. is personally productive because of the emotional payoff, or as I call it, "enjoyment response," that they provide to their participants; the "thrill of victory" and the "agony of defeat," respectively speaking. And I leave room for the possibility (as mentioned earlier) that such emotional responses in regard to game-playing may be an expression of the soul. But I also feel compelled to say at this time in regard to this theory (even at the risk of being labeled "sexist"), that these game-related enjoyment responses are seemingly more profoundly expressed through the souls of men rather than through those of women, generally speaking (and for whatever reason).

To me, the three most fascinating human enjoyment responses that I've witnessed are (1) when women swoon over male musicians, such as was first reported in the late 1800's when Franz Liszt performed piano concerts, with the ensuing female responses becoming entitled "Liszt-omania," and with said female response characteristic being capitalized upon by Western culture ever since; (2) the human (and as I just mentioned, mostly male) response to video-gaming, which reared its "pixilated" head around 1980 and hasn't shown any signs of letting up since, wherein "gamers" are able to play for practically unceasing amounts of time. The human gambling response is probably a manifestation of this self-same mechanism within the brain as is this video-gaming response. And (3) the male response to female nudity, which catapults the male sex response into overdrive. What a strong and valuable tool for human behavioral research the internet has become when it can reveal such information/statistics such as how practically any one of the hundreds of thousands of porn videos that are available for viewing on the world-wide-web often have over a hundred-thousand separate individual viewings attached to each one of them. This statistic suggests that practically all of the males in the world who have internet access (and probably a lot of the females, too) are viewing a lot of porn on a practically daily basis (and "yes," the only way that I could be privy to such statistics would be if I myself were to have visited a lot of porn sites. Who asked you? Just kidding.)

Jobs that involve play are extremely gratifying to their performers. Any "successful performance" in a field of play will provide any of its players with a commensurately more immense feeling of exhilaration and gratification than would its equivalent counterpart in any other given field. Why is this? Again, it may have to do with the nature of our souls. When we play, we are most alive. Henry David Thoreau wrote, "Children, who play life, discern its true law and relations more clearly than men...." And Jesus states in the New Testament that only children and those adults who manage to maintain childlike qualities or childlike innocence in life are capable of constituting the population of Heaven. And the suspicion that our consciences esteem the act of play is corroborated by the fact that professions that are designed around play are some of the most lucrative in the world. You don't see people lining up and paying good money to see other people perform labor or to watch them serve one another, do you? In the movie *Rounders,* Matt Damon's character, upon having played poker for the first time in six months, stated afterwards that, "I felt alive for the first time in six months." And along these same lines, I don't believe any pro athletes when they state that the aspect of their profession that they're going to miss the most upon their imminent retirement is going to be the camaraderie that they've shared with their fellow teammates. This is disingenuous. What they're really going to miss is the self-gratification and fan adulation that they received whenever they had a successful performance in whatever respective field of competition they were involved in.

Activities to which women seem to have the greater emotional or "soul response" than men seem to me to revolve more around the act of "going": *going* out for drinks, *going* out to dinner, *going* shopping, *going* to the beach, *going* on a cruise, *going* to a different city (traveling), *going* sightseeing, *going* camping, *going* to a party, *going* to the movies, *going* to a concert, *going* to a dance club. Apparently, for a woman to be relegated to having to spend her free time in a restricted environment is a cruel fate for any of them to have to endure. This leads me to suspect that prison might be for women, emotionally speaking, a more debilitating environment for them to be exposed to than it is for men (except for when you consider the possibility for male rape to occur in the male prisons, that is).

Would anyone argue against the fact that in our own Western society, as people gradually age, they're expected to gradually wean themselves away from their collective focuses on a "play-centered" lifestyle in deference towards an acceptance of, and focus towards, a lifestyle that becomes gradually more and more centered around the concept of "responsibility"? I think not. The philosophically-related questions to these arguments then are these: is this transitional aspect of human maturation the ideal, or at least the *unavoidable*, scenario? Probably. And, if so, need it be that gratification of our own individual souls be sacrificed in subjugation to the propagation of our society's needs? Probably, as well. Or could it be the case, perhaps, that fulfilling one's adult-oriented responsibilities can become as gratifying to our adult souls as playing had once proven itself to be to our childhood souls? I doubt it, since I've never heard of any professional adult game-players who've complained about *their* lives, while I *have* heard some complaints from the remaining adult population regarding *their* careers. Also, there's the previously mentioned argument that our souls never change from childhood to adulthood.

Becoming a disciplined and responsible member of society is obviously a necessary trait for humans to adopt, but I say shove as much play in between the cracks of discipline and responsibility as is humanly possible. It's okay for adults to play more, as far as I'm concerned. For years, I felt that the song that I most identified with was "Teacher" by Jethro Tull, because I considered myself a teacher at heart; not realizing until recently that this "Teacher" and I shared the same fundamental message that was voiced in that song: "Jump up, look around, find yourself some fun...." Now, as a result of noticing this philosophical similarity between the two of us, I've become an even bigger fan than I already was of the work of Ian Anderson (of Jethro Tull).

Earlier, I conjectured how our souls could be considered sacred. But because most game-playing participants (and probably the entire game-playing public at large, for that matter) fail to see this possible connection between game-play and the gratification of the soul, the participants in such activities often provide a disservice to the game that they're playing, and to themselves, as well, and also to those around them, whenever one of them happens to selfishly express his or her disapproval over losing a contest; not realizing, and therefore subsequently taking for granted, the privilege that it is to merely be allowed to engage in what amounts to being potentially sacred activity.

I believe that physical exercise is personally productive because without it, your health deteriorates. And you can't be happy unless you're healthy. Any day in which a person forces his or her heart and lungs to pump greater supplies of blood and oxygen to his or her muscles due to his or her performance of physical exercise is a productive one, regardless of the lack of productivity that the rest of the day may hold for him or her. Any muscles that are forced to work harder will achieve increased productivity. To me, physical exercise is more important than mental exercise. One reason for this belief is that the mind is of little use if there's no body there to support it, which would also essentially be the case if a person were in physical pain or discomfort all of the time. The unfathomable mental gymnastics that are required by the mind to simultaneously conceive, construct, animate, and direct our nightly dream sequences and sessions implies to me that our brains get plenty of regular exercise simply from this activity. Through the use of dreams, our subconscious is also given a means by which to deal with stressful issues in our lives, which also benefits our health. It seems counterintuitive, however, that our brains are provided with their most rest while we're dreaming, because that's apparently the period of time when our brains become the most active. Along these same lines, our eyes get their most rest during the "rapid eye movement" period of sleep, but this is also the period of time in which our eye muscles are at *their* most active level. To get back to exercise, though, almost all of us will naturally engage in mental exercise throughout the course of daily living through such simple acts as interacting and communicating with other people and navigating our cars in and out of traffic amidst our many roadways. But physical exercise requires a distinct, concerted effort on our parts in order for us to reap its benefits. I hate working out, but my conscience "guilts" me into doing it because my brain recognizes its value.

Espousing philosophy may be socially beneficial, but making love is much more personally gratifying. Physical romance is personally productive because the heart craves it, perhaps even literally so, as scientific studies have concluded that there's a correlation between individuals who remain "single" and their relatively early demises as compared with their potential married counterparts. I'd venture to say that practically every adult male would freely admit that their respective positive sexual encounters would rank as the greatest experiences of their lives. That's why it's always worthwhile to ask a child what his or her greatest experience may have been up until that point in his or her life because their answers will vary, but it's a rather pointless endeavor to ask the same question of an adult male because practically all adult males' responses would be relatively the same: their answers would revolve around sex. Sex can be considered the Cadillac or Led Zeppelin or Michael Jordan (whichever model of excellence you prefer) of male activities. I admit that I've only engaged in projects such as the one that you're currently engaged in reading as a result of myself practically never having a female around with which to occupy my time and attention.

Drinking alcohol and doing drugs apparently makes most people happy, as these drugs' effects seem to increase the enjoyment of practically any activity for these people. I personally "get no kick from champagne. Mere alcohol doesn't thrill me at all" (as borrowed from the Cole Porter song, "I Get a Kick Out of You"). God himself states his affinity for alcohol in the Old Testament. I suspect there's little reason to categorically separate alcohol use from other forms of drug use, though, as they both share the same intent and purpose: making people feel better. The only worthwhile comment in the entire movie *Benjamin Button* (a rather pointless endeavor

31

in which Brad Pitt's character aged backwards) was that everywhere Benjamin went in the world, everyone drank alcohol. Apparently, drinking and drugging is as much a part of the human experience as breathing is. It's the moderation of these activities that seems to cause people the most trouble, though. It seems that as long as people have "drinking money" at their disposal, hardly any of them will ever consider their lives to be *that* bad. Alcohol and drugs are an analgesic for practically any form of misery. But once a person becomes drunk, that person can practically no longer even be considered a human being. His or her brain no longer functions as a normal human's would, and any attempt at communication with anyone in such a state is invariably rendered pointless. Not to mention the expense that all of these recreational-type drugs incur on our population's collective annual budgets. Along with this alcoholic expense, expensive domiciles and "eating out" are about the most wasteful monetary expenditures that I can think of. So much more of our population would have the freedom to invest significant portions of their incomes towards their respective dreams if they would drink less, live in smaller homes, and cook their own dinners. But who knows, maybe drinking, living in a nice home, and eating out constitutes, to a large extent, the overall extent of most people's dreams.

If Hollywood deathbed confessions and New Testament doctrine are any indication, then cultivating relationships with loved ones is one of the most important activities that a person can engage in in life. I personally have trouble developing strong feelings for, or attachments with, friends and family, though, for whatever reason, so my productivity potential in this regard seems limited. But for everyone else who feels like friendship is an important aspect of life for them, I encourage them to somehow figure out how to make more time to continue cultivating friendships whenever and however they possibly can should they at any time happen to feel like it's a deficient aspect of any of their respective lives. But don't just do it over the phone, for goodness' sake. "Catching up" with people on the phone is an unsatisfactory experience in my opinion. I think that we should either make an effort to visit with people face-to-face or relegate ourselves to not catching up with them at all.

Child-rearing, like teaching, should probably be considered personally productive because the parent is shaping a young person's heart and mind, and that seems like it would be a gratifying accomplishment for anyone to make. I suspect that in most cases, progeny are a reflection of their parents' parenting skill. Shouldn't it become every father's intention to make his child the greatest human alive (in a moral sense)? And if every teacher treated every student as if each child were his or her own offspring, it could then, by corollary, become every teacher's intention to try to make every student the greatest human alive. Teaching and coaching isn't unrewarding work, but it must be noted that watching others perform pales in comparison to the exhilaration one feels through performing one's own self.

Creating art is probably personally productive. I imagine that it's the "creativity" aspect of art that attracts people to it. There's apparently something very appealing to our souls about "creating" something. This suggests to me that expanding or exercising the creative aspects of our minds is a means towards becoming closer to divinity. Playing music, to me, is probably doubly productive because one is both "creating" and "playing" at the same time.

I've heard that "helping others" is very rewarding. Personally, if the circumstances could have arisen in my life wherein the people that I've had the occasions to have helped over the years never would have actually had needed my help in the first place, then I would have preferred that circumstance as compared to the one in which I was compelled to help them in the first place. Like I mentioned before as in my sentiments regarding work, I've failed to experience the dignity that's purported to accompany "helping others." Such admissions as these may end up being an indictment of my own character, but I'm more interested in knowing the truth about myself than trying to project myself as being some sort of a humanitarian.

So, by using these above-presented standards as a guideline, what could one now anticipate an entirely productive life to look like? By my definition, complete productivity is commensurate to doing just what your brain and soul together suggest that you do and avoiding everything else; with the presumed feeling of satisfaction that would naturally accompany such an act of obedience on a person's part being present, as well. But put into a more pragmatic sense, I feel like everyone should just do whatever it takes in life to keep themselves from either killing themselves or going insane. One possible standard by which to potentially guide your life is that if you aren't experiencing the same exciting occurrences that generally transpire in the respective books and movies that you happen to come across throughout the course of your life, then life is probably passing you by.

Pragmatic Teaching

I believe that the proper future for all of society's institutions, such as education, religion, and family, lies in/with "getting real" with one another and the abandonment of formality in our exchange of ideas with one another. "No holds barred" openness and honesty is the only way to have an unencumbered learning environment. Only when all possible questions and concerns have been addressed can complete understanding be achieved.

The most important part about being a teacher is for the teacher to establish and then maintain dominance or control over the students. Every teacher must approach each work day as if going to war, because every teacher must be prepared to confront any and all challenges to his or her authority with which he or she may be confronted throughout the course of any given work day. In a best-case scenario for a teacher in his or her work environment, he or she will be able to inspire some students to greatness. In a worst-case scenario for a teacher in his or her work environment, he or she will "prevent the inmates from running the asylum."

After the teacher's authority is established, the next most important thing to establish between the teacher and the student is trust. Trust is necessary in order for the "lead-follow" dynamic between the two of them to develop and work. If the student trusts that the teacher has his or her best interests at heart, then the student will "buy in" to the teacher's efforts. If the student is suspicious of the teacher's motivation, then the student will be unwilling to cooperate with the teacher's direction.

There's only one correct way to teach. That's *through* the eyes of the teacher and *to* the eyes of the student. The teacher explains the world as he or she sees it and nothing more. But the student's point of view must be considered, understood, and accounted for when delivering the educational message. When the message is properly delivered to the student, the student will eventually know everything that the teacher knows, plus, along the way in life, the student will inherently learn things that the teacher doesn't know. This process provides the backdrop for the student's assumption towards his or her role as the eventual teacher.

Teaching, like parenting, is simply making judgment call after judgment call, day after day. Minor situations arise every day for teachers in which there are no set protocols for how to deal with them. The teacher is left to his or her own devices as far as coming up with viable options for solving any student-related problems with which he or she is confronted, and is likewise left to his or her own wits as far as anticipating the likely results of the implementation of any of those options. The teacher then goes with his or her best guess regarding how to deal with the particular situation and then learns from the experience. Over time, through the process of trial and error, experienced teachers learn how to successfully deal with practically any situation that they could possibly be faced with. And that's why experienced teachers get paid more than beginning teachers.

There's much debate in our modern society as to which methodology is more effective in disciplining a child: corporal punishment or rewards-based reinforcement (the granting of such, the withholding of such, or the removal of such). From my gleanings, the psychological community (the community that presumes to understand the long-term effects of both methods) seems to be of the mindset that favors the latter. The man the Bible purports to be "the wisest man ever" (Solomon), favored the former. I've never had any children, so my opinion on this matter would have to be formed from a strictly a priori point of view, which I'm not in favor of doing. But it certainly seems reasonable to me to physically hurt children until they can understand reason, at any rate.

Pragmatic Education

Discipline is making yourself do something that you don't want to do. The discipline that's required for a student to wake up early and be both still and quiet for hours on end in his or her respective classrooms, and for him or her to then have to pay attention and do written assignments associated with subject areas in which he or she likely has little to no interest, is arguably as valuable as any of the knowledge that that child will actually receive from any of the specific subject matter with which he or she is presented in any of those classrooms themselves. Being forced out of sleep in the morning because it's time to wake up is one of life's most wretched sensations. Then there's the agony of homework. No wonder I still sometimes have nightmares about being in school. But I'm neither questioning the methodology nor the curriculum that's presented in our school systems. I can see the value in all of the presented subject matter, as well as the value of the coinciding workloads that are attached to them. School is a necessary evil. But then again, I would also consider schools to be worthwhile investments on our society's part even if they provided no other service than to keep those brats off the streets and out of adults' hair for the large portion of the day, which I'm happy to say that they still manage to accomplish to this day.

Can you imagine how fun it was for me to have a full complement of my peers available with whom to play football, baseball, or basketball games during school every day in P.E. class? Plus, we were allowed to be our own bosses during those games. There weren't any "head coaches" around to tell us how we had to do things. We played the games the way we wanted to, and the activities sold themselves. I would've been willing to pay money to participate in P.E. class every day, as long as we still would have been able to have picked the activities. What I believe P.E. should mean for the student is a brief opportunity during the school day for him or her to engage in the wholesome indulgence of his or her own soul. The activities that have been traditionally offered in P.E. classes are a privilege to be engaged in, but that doesn't mean that I feel any of those activities should be forced down any students' throats, though. If some students would prefer to use their P.E. time simply as a "recess" time to spend conversing with their classmates, away from the drudgery of their other class work, then that would be fine with me, too. Maybe such activity (or lack thereof) is a more fulfilling use of those particular students' time as far as their particular souls are concerned. I don't believe that learning the activities that are presented in P.E. classes are as important for students to learn as the core subjects they're mandated to take during the remainder of their school days. I prefer seeing P.E. class as a place where everyone can look forward to heading, like a sanctuary, regardless of each student's anticipated level of participation in any of the given activities that are presented there. And I believe that any feelings of enjoyment that any student receives from attending P.E. class can later be transformed by him or her into feelings of respect towards becoming active and participating in sports later on in his or her own life.

As far as student behavior policy is concerned, I don't see any reason why students should be allowed to talk while they're at school. Kids today talk too much as it is, as far as I'm concerned. But once a child demonstrates that he or she is completely and fully socialized, though, I don't see any reason why he or she shouldn't be treated with the same dignity and respect that adults have come to expect to receive from one another. Ideally, the time at which actualized socialization occurs within the student would be the point at which that student would begin to be treated like an adult not at some required, arbitrary calendar year, as is presently the case.

College liberal arts programs are just more of the same of what's provided for in the childhood education systems. I never learned anything useful in any of *my* college classes. Learning history only serves to provide perspective on how normal vs. abnormal any occurrence is. The most significant historical fact to all of our lives that history has to teach us is that in a best-case scenario, humans get about eighty good years to do something worthwhile with their lives, and that throughout the course of each of our respective adulthoods, our collective health will continue to deteriorate. History can provide models of success or failure for anyone interested in trying to rule the world, but nothing much more useful beyond that for the common man to glean.

Ray Santoli

Penmanship is a revealing art form as far as I'm concerned, and I believe that handwriting analysis would be a worthwhile subject for schools to offer to students as well, as I feel there's a relationship between the aesthetics of a person's handwriting and his or her cognitive function. When executed correctly, the written language is beautiful to look at, especially the scripted form. Within this same subject area, the correct handgrip on the writing implement should be emphasized, as either the accurate or mistaken application of this fundamental skill can, I believe, make a strong statement about the level of a person's education. Also worth noting on this subject is pen quality. Ball point pens are an affront to human dignity as far as I'm concerned. And the fact that pen quality is even an issue in this day and age is also a travesty in my eyes. I could practically pull out what little amount of hair I have left on my head over the poor quality of pens that I've been continuously subjected to using throughout the course of my life. I hope that all of the pen manufacturers out there are at least getting rich from the lack of quality that I suspect they're *intentionally* withholding from their pen supplies. Somebody please tell me where I can get a pen that dispenses a liberal amount of ink per stroke and that also has a smooth, fluid response to it, so that I can buy a ton of them, because I'm sure that if I were to ever own such a pen, my quality of penmanship would greatly improve.

A person's use of grammar is also revealing. The use of poor grammar reflects if not a lack of intelligence, at least a lack of effort on a person's part, because everyone receives the same grammatical education in this country. So there's no reason for anyone to be completely ignorant on the subject.

It's a rather surprising fact to me that teachers in our country's public school systems are given such latitude with which to teach their given subjects. This freedom can potentially produce large discrepancies in some subject areas as to the quality of education that's provided to the students. I'm surprised that the curriculums haven't become more nationally uniform by this seemingly late date and time in our country's educational history.

Pragmatic Science

One would think that performing scientific studies would be a productive activity in which to engage, but traditionally, the conclusions that studies reach rarely result in a definitive application that can help improve a person's quality of life, because it usually takes a combination of information gleaned from years of research and a multitude of studies to produce just one useful theory. One of the most useful theories that I've ever encountered, though, is the one that suggests that human offspring are so different from their parents due to the fact that certain genes can sometimes "skip a generation." This theory alone has provided for a multitude of explanations to mysteries that I've encountered regarding my own life.

In the field of physics, the dichotomy that's demonstrated between the laws that govern quantum mechanics vs. the laws that govern larger scale physics also works in harmony with the Eastern philosophical "yin-yang" model of existence (where every phenomenon has its opposite): randomness vs. order, respectively. Quantum mechanics has been proven to be exceedingly random, while large scale physics operates following elegantly simple equations. This perhaps "designed-in" dichotomy is what may be stifling the discovery of a unified field theory that would unite these two fields of physics. I believe that the cosmology field's unified assertion that "dark matter exists" will eventually prove to be a black eye on that field's reputation, as I suspect that that assertion is spurious. Just as scientists failed to properly calculate the mechanics of bumblebee flight for years, leading them to their collective failed conjecture that bumblebees shouldn't be able to fly, until they finally got the calculations right not too long ago and realized that bumblebees *could* theoretically fly. I suspect this present-day community of cosmologists, as well, is going to be left with egg on their collective faces when they realize it isn't "dark matter" that needs to be calculated into their equations for figuring out why galaxies spin at the rates that they do, it's something else.

If the *Dr. Phil Show* is any indication (and I think it is), there seems to have been some worthwhile advancements in the field of psychology over the years. The ability to identify the motivation behind human behavior seems to have become a science. And what a worthwhile science it is. I suggest implementing this "understanding human behavior" curriculum into our school systems at as early a stage as possible, and with nonstop progression in the subject area in mind for all of its students as well. I know *I* would certainly like to always know the exact reasons why I and everyone else say and do the things that we do.

I don't doubt that evolution within different species of animals has ever occurred. But something weird, that's without scientific explanation, is going on all around us: the concept of animal instinct is at odds with the evolutionary principle of adaptation through means of genetic mutation. Instinctive behavior occurs independently of an animal's ability to "figure out" how or why it's to perform these acts.

Genes can't generate specific behaviors. They can only generate general behaviors. There's no explanation for a helpless newborn's ability to "seek out" a nipple for which to latch onto; or for an animal's subconscious avoidance of breeding within its own family; or for tiny-brained animals to be able to create architecturally advanced domiciles for themselves to dwell in. In the hierarchy of behavioral ability, first there's an animal's ability to imitate a behavior that they observe; next, there's an animal's ability to figure out a behavior to perform through a combination of reasoning and trial and error. Instinct skips both of these steps. Animals (including humans) are neither imitating one another through observation, nor are they figuring out for themselves why they should perform whatever "instinctive" behavior they may be carrying out. They're just *doing it somehow*, anyway. It's basically magic when you think about it. If such behaviors as these instinctive ones can just somehow spontaneously occur into our existence, then practically any behavior is possible. Instinct is a concept of "random smarts," and because it's a reality without the hope of any scientific explanation, I think that its presence suggests that supernatural forces have been at play in the development of our existence.

Human resiliency is surprisingly strong. Millions of people lose their jobs and don't have any money, but they almost always still somehow survive. People are all of the time befallen by misfortune, but they almost always seem to be able to persevere. Potentially devastating life obstacles are often thrown in people's paths, but they almost always seem to be able to manage them. Practically anybody can manage this world for a little while, but I'm amazed at how practically everybody seems to be able to manage it for their entire lives. The demand for money never ceases, and once a person is out of money, his or her problems only become compounded at that point. The snowball effect from such a situation should have a catastrophic effect on their lives, but it often doesn't, somehow. I suspect that relatives, friends, church organizations, and government programs are greatly responsible for picking up much of the slack in many of these cases. Along these lines, I'm surprised the elements don't have a greater effect on human mortality rates. Our bodies can't handle much deviation in ambient temperature. The rate of death due to exposure seems to me like it should be much higher than it is. Or perhaps, like suicide rates, it's just that these are the type of statistics that media groups prefer to refrain from divulging to the public. Maybe it's bad for our morale for us to hear about such occurrences.

Pragmatic Spirituality/Religion

I have to assume that any activity that promotes spiritual growth (if such a thing is even possible) is personally productive because it perhaps changes how one feels or changes one's perspective on life. Though, again, I have to say I've never personally experienced anything that's changed the way I feel or has changed my perspective on life. I've often hoped to receive some sort of sign of confirmation, or support, or encouragement, or direction from the universe at large or the powers that be. I've hoped to somehow enter into an altered state of consciousness that leads me towards a definitive direction in life, instead of maintaining the uncertainty of this seemingly meaningless existence that I've had the frustration of experiencing my whole life. The so-called phenomenon of "synchronicity," in which seemingly *unrelated* events suddenly seem to become *related* to one another due to their simultaneous occurrence and some shared link between the two of them, is considered to be a form of this type of spiritual feedback to which I'm referring. Common examples of synchronicity are when two individuals, independently of one another, mention the same obscure word or phrase within a short period of time of one another, or when you're reading something and the television or the radio in the background mentions the same phrase that you happen to be reading at that very moment. Synchronicity theory suggests that coincidences such as these are not strictly coincidental, and that these occurrences should be construed by the individuals who experience them as evidence or external affirmation that they are on the right track with whatever endeavor they happen to be pursuing at the time of these coincidences. But the support of such a theory seemingly places one at odds with the Bible's precept of adhering to a strictly God-based reliance on direction for one's life.

Astrology can probably be placed in the same holistic/counter-culture/alternative/new age/pseudo or whatever you want to call it category of science that synchronicity would be placed in because it also lacks scientific credibility, due to the fact that it hasn't been able to accurately or reliably reproduce lab results regarding its purported spiritually-related power of prediction. But just as with synchronicity, there seem to be some statistically significant coincidences associated with astrology that prompt me to be unwilling to dismiss the possibility that astrology has something of value to offer to us. Although I've neither seen nor heard any evidence to suggest that there's any accurate predictive quality associated with astrology as far as its ability to anticipate future events in individuals' lives is concerned, the statistically significant coincidental aspect of astrology to me lies in how it can accurately label/chart individuals' personality characteristics based on no more information than an individual's simple birth date. It's an intriguing source of cocktail lounge entertainment for me to conduct informal scientific investigations into the accuracy of these astrologically-predicted personality characteristics with people whom I meet. As far as the methodology of this lounge investigation goes, the predicted personality characteristics that are associated with the bar patron's zodiac sign are "Googled," and I then see if that person actually agrees with whatever personality characteristics astrology seemingly predicts that he or she will actually be in possession of. Generally speaking, most people find the similarities of the "personality characteristics astrology predicts that they will possess" vs. the "personality characteristics they actually feel like they possess" to be "uncanny" in its accuracy. And this extremely high level of accuracy has also been my own personal experience in regard to these astrologically-predicted personality characteristics, as well.

Skepticism regarding the level of scientific accuracy that can be associated or attributed to these personality characteristics needs to be addressed. Personality characteristics can be hard to define and also subject to an individual's perception and prejudices. In other words, in regard to personality characteristic perceptions and definitions, it should first be determined if each personality characteristic means the same thing to each person tested. This variable is never accounted for in testing, though, and such a source of potential unreliability has to be considered when drawing conclusions regarding this type of inquiry. The "prejudices" aspect of the equation has to be addressed thusly: there's the possibility that people are agreeing with the personality characteristics that astrology proposes for them simply because they *want* their personalities to be in agreement with the astrological predictions. This potential source of unreliability also has to be considered when drawing conclusions regarding this type of inquiry. But I believe the overwhelming degree of personal agreement between individuals and the corresponding personality characteristics that astrology predicts for them makes up for the margin of error that discrepancies in definitions, perceptions, and prejudices might provide. But, of course, I could be wrong.

Predicting personality characteristics is a difficult, or at least odd, field of inquiry to consider when you think about it. I mean, what could astrology's mechanism possibly be for predicting these personality characteristics? For any scientifically-based personality studies to be performed, there would naturally have to be an aspect of observation that would be included in the research, as well as extensive data gathering regarding the individual's heredity history and all of the environmental circumstances to which the individual had been exposed throughout his or her life (this is "nature" and "nurture" data). But astrology predicts how people are going to feel and act before they're even born and without any data collection at all regarding the individual besides that of the individual's birth date. And due to the fact that science is unable to come up with any means of its own as far as duplicating this astrological feat of prenatal personality characteristic identification, and also due to astrology's apparent high level of accuracy in this regard, these facts seem to suggest to me that just as in the subject of animal instinct, there's a supernatural origin associated with the development of this phenomenon.

To continue with the question of the veracity of astrology's ability to predict everyone's personality characteristics, no one can know how another person feels. Conclusions about another person's feelings can only be drawn after having observed the behavior of that particular person. And I'll grant that there can be a strong degree of reliability attached to such observation-based conclusions whenever the observations are conducted by psychological experts. But since I wouldn't be able to definitively answer personality-based questions regarding another person, I'll simply provide my own personal responses regarding the astrologically-predicted personality characteristics of my own zodiac sign, "Aquarius." Leading astrological website sources are in agreement that Aquarians are generally in possession of the following personality characteristics that I also feel I'm likely in possession of, such as: being friendly, loyal, easygoing, logical, practical, future-minded, big picture-minded, communicative, stubborn, unemotional, self-centered, and perhaps even a bit of a know-it-all. And upon becoming reacquainted once again with these apparently (according to astrology) *unavoidable* traits that I'm subject to possessing, I'm led to the conclusion that this very book itself is the quintessential Aquarian project, as it contains prototypical Aquarian subject matter/content that's presented in a prototypically Aquarian manner. In fact, I can't help but now get the impression that my whole life may have been less a matter of choice on my part, and more of an act of destiny on astrology's part, given the apparent unavoidable inclinations of action that someone such as myself, who happens to be born in early February, is astrologically conditioned to choose. "And it's marvelous in my sight," to quote the Bible.

If there is a God, his influence in our lives and in this world is somewhere between 0 percent and 100 percent. What would 0 percent look like? In other words, what would our world look like were it to be free from God's influence? I believe it would look much, if not *exactly*, the same as it does now. What would 100 percent influence entail? That human freedom of choice were an illusion and that God were really the decision-maker and operator in every situation. *That* certainly doesn't seem like it's the case, though, does it? Many years ago, I thought I had an original notion when I suggested to myself that God existed, but that he no longer involved himself in our lives or in the day-to-day functioning of this world. I soon learned, however, that others had also come to this conclusion centuries ago, and that they had called themselves "deists." Apparently, some of America's founding fathers were some of them.

Here's a Christian axiom that I've been hearing for years, but one that I don't find acceptable: "God is good all the time." "Good" as demonstrated by what actions, though? "God's reasons are beyond our understanding." That seems like an acceptable axiom to me. "Giving all the glory of good things to God." That also seems like an acceptable axiom to me. But don't give credit where credit isn't due. The only way that God could be considered good all of the time is in a purely detached sense. As in he's up in heaven not misbehaving up there. But once he and his supposed powers are attached to this world, I don't see how he can any longer be credited with being good all of the time. Theoretically, he has the power to prevent injustices here on earth, yet injustices occur all of the time on his theoretical watch. "God is good on Judgment Day" seems like it might be a much more appropriate saying.

I, personally, only prefer to associate with Christians who acknowledge the possibility that they still may be going to Hell in spite of their admitted belief in the validity of the Christian message. These would be persons who freely acknowledge the possibility that their lives are *not* okay in God's eyes, and that they're *not* going to get away with having led such lives on Judgment Day. It's only acceptable to me for a Christian to have an alternative attitude to this "hell bound" anticipation if said Christian's life, through repeated painstaking effort on his or her own part, is clearly discernable from those of the "unwashed masses" in terms of his or her dedication and devotion to maintenance of all of the Christian principles that are set forth in the New Testament.

Our Christian society's collective practice of taking personal offense at any of their own happened exposure to any and all forms of obscenity is misbegotten, I believe. To my way of understanding New Testament scripture, God's the only one who's obliged to take umbrage with any such transgressions, while, for their own parts, Christians are directed to remain spiritually unaffected by any such exposure to such transgressions.

If there are any Christians out there who are in possession of any of the "gifts of the spirit" such as healing, speaking in foreign tongues, prophecy, etc., such cases should be scientifically documented in order to finally put to an end the question of whether or not the gifts of the spirit are currently in existence or not, once and for all. The fact that I haven't heard of any scientifically documented cases leads me to believe that there aren't any people out there who still possess any of the gifts of the spirit.

Pragmatic Art

I feel like I've seen all of the good movies and heard all of the good songs. Sometimes I wish I would be hypnotized into forgetting all of them so I could experience the enjoyment of experiencing them all for the first time again, which I'm assuming would subsequently improve my quality of life. I've never enjoyed reading that much, so I don't generally share the same sentiment regarding novels or poetry, though. But I'd still like to provide my own definition of poetry, however: poetry is the harmonic expression of parts, the product of which expands knowledge; as opposed to simple art and beauty, which is harmonic, but lacks the aspect of knowledge expansion. It's worth noting, of course, that poetry can theoretically occur in any field of endeavor.

What good are great poems or paintings if hardly anyone understands why they're so? This deprivation of explanation suggests to me there's been a deficiency in the field of art education. If certain works of art truly are great, then it should be clearly explained to everyone why they're so. There continues to be a seemingly unnecessary chasm between those who know and those who don't. Greatness without an explanation as to why it's great is useless. I also feel the art world is operating under a misconception that *all* talented artists' work should be highly valued. But I propose that only the *first* piece of art that demonstrates a new style or approach to art should be highly valued, as everything else that's done in that same vein beyond that original work is merely an imitation of that original concept. Once photography was invented about 150 years ago, the medium of paint seems to have become an all but irrelevant or obsolete means of depicting the world around us, anyways.

I find the widespread popularity of tattoos in our society to be a rather surprising trend, as the images generally tend to be nothing more than the type of pictures and designs that thirteen-year-old boys doodle in their classrooms. And you don't often hear the fellow students of such individuals voicing any desires to have such images indelibly drawn onto their skins, do you? I'd deem such artwork to be certainly worthy of magnetic affixture to kitchen appliances, but hardly much more.

The film *Dead Poets Society* referred to personal activities that "suck the marrow out of life." This is the self-same concept to which I've been referring and to which I also believe that our species should seemingly aspire. All of the activities that I mentioned in the "Pragmatic Lifestyle" chapter improve a person's quality of life, and I would consider most of them to be "marrow-sucking" activities. But although *Dead Poets Society* touched upon this pragmatic theme, it failed to linger there. For the most part in our cinematic history, filmmakers have shortchanged themselves and the viewing public with pointless movie scripts. A film is a tremendous opportunity to share a message, but that opportunity has been all but squandered by our film industry. Do you know how to tell if a movie is great? There will be a spontaneous eruption of applause from the audience following its conclusion. Books of fiction are generally guilty of the same crime as the film industry. If our society ever figures out a philosophically sound approach to life, then trivial pursuits such as reading fiction would seem more justifiable, but our society still wanders around aimlessly even up to this seemingly late stage in our history.

The daily news broadcasts are generally useless, as well. The only time they have anything worthwhile to say is whenever they interrupt other programming in order to provide information with their "emergency broadcasts." But one productive service that newscasts *do* provide is to keep businessmen honest through the prospect of providing negative publicity. The "talking head" journalists associated with these broadcasts always seem to display an air of phony concern to me that I (and I hope most others) find to be "off-putting." They're "acting" as much as any Broadway star, but much less convincingly, I'm afraid to say. Since local broadcasts represent specific regions of a country and national broadcasts represent an entire country itself, I don't see why the producers of such broadcasts don't hire the most attractive hosts possible to read the teleprompters, because if they were to do so, it would allow each respective region or country to literally, "put its best face forward." The same goes for Hollywood. Why don't TV and movie producers simply hire the most attractive actresses available to fill all of the available female roles? Even though it's a bit of an understatement, all that actors basically have to do for their jobs is to recite lines of dialogue and feign emotions. Wouldn't it make more sense, and wouldn't we all consequently enjoy these two forms of media much more, if it were left strictly to "the beautiful people" to fulfill those duties?

There's a visceral response to music. It affects us. It's the artistic mode of greatest potential impact on its listener. Poems affect us, too, but to a lesser degree; and paintings, as well, to a still lesser degree. Hearing a song is an actual experience. That's how and why music connects people—through a shared experience. The musical experience is enhanced whenever it's shared. And music apparently affects everyone the same way. The only difference between people's musical experience is the taste/appeal of different genres of music. A person's taste in music is revealing because it demonstrates whether or not that person is capable of discerning between "good" and "great." Whenever people choose to expose their taste in music to the rest of the world by playing songs on a jukebox, it's a form of audial hijacking for whoever also has to listen to it. If you happen to be in the audience in such a scenario, you just have to hope that you and whoever is playing the jukebox have similar tastes. And boy, is that rare.

As a rule of thumb, I believe a listener has to be exposed to a song at least ten times before he or she should be expected to fully appreciate a song's worth. Noels/carols are by far the best Christian type songs. I believe the musical fruit produced by western culture's modern brand of Christianity is a testimony to its impotency/inferiority. It's terrible. "Barbershop" style singing is special because of the "extra" sounding voice that it's able to produce. It's perhaps a style designed *by* God to be performed *for* God.

Fashion choices are also revealing, to the extent that they can reveal when a person is out-of-touch with the common sentiment. Also, when a person's color choices fail to coordinate within his or her ensemble, there's rarely an excuse for that. I mean, what are some people thinking by putting some of those colors and fabrics together? Are they blind? But if they don't mind, I guess I don't either. Credit is of course due to anyone who can come up with an unusual look and still manage to "make it work" for him or herself. For my money, the eighteenth century was our culture's pinnacle as far as fashion achievement is concerned. Fashion's been in retrograde ever since then. The lengthy, bright, primary-colored jackets that they wore with those large metallic buttons sewn in to them, with big cuffs at the ends of the sleeves, and with overlapping lapels has failed to be surpassed in aesthetic value in my opinion. And the piece de resistance to the ensemble was the frilly neckerchief called a jabot and the lace cuffs at the ends of the undershirts that protruded beyond the jacket's sleeves. Although I think this era missed the mark with their knickers, black buckle shoes, and white powdered wigs, the jacket ensemble still places the colonial era as head and shoulders above any other fashion era in my opinion.

I have no doubt it's good for the soul to sing, as my experience with live karaoke has told me. And it's this perhaps spiritual aspect of singing that I feel cements karaoke's current and future popularity as a recreational attraction to the masses. I'd also venture to say that it's probably good for the soul to dance as well, but dancing is such a feminine activity that it's no wonder heterosexual men are so self-conscious about engaging in it. Let alone the fact that most of us men do it so poorly. Break-dancing is the most impressive form of dance to me because of its use of imagery. Flamenco dancing is the second-most impressive form to me because of the advanced rhythms that its dancers are able to produce with their boots. And it's also for that reason, to me, that flamenco dancing is probably the most difficult form of dance to learn and therefore perform. The best thing for men about dancing is that women are attracted to men who can dance. Related to that, I suspect that women would have a more enjoyable experience were they to go to see "fully-clothed" male dance revue shows rather than going to see "stripper-style" male dance revue shows. Women aren't interested in seeing dancing that focuses on men's private parts. I suspect that men's private parts are more of a "turn-off" than a "turn-on" for them. I believe most women have sex with men *in spite* of the so-called attractiveness of the male form rather than *because* of it. This supposed fact that the male form is unattractive to females leads me to conclude that the irony of the story of *Beauty and the Beast* is that a story such as that could actually occur. As I believe has been shown in many studies, men are extremely visual in their attraction towards the opposite sex, but women aren't. The fact that a male might be rather repulsive to look at, though likely an initially significant factor in the eyes of a female, I feel, could easily become a dismissible one later on for her.

"Child naming" is a supernatural art form or skill in my own mind. Parents almost always seem to pick the appropriate name for their children. Evidence of this is when you come across someone in life who reminds you of someone else whom you've met or known, and behold, it turns out that the two of them both share the same name. I've experienced this phenomenon too many times in my life for myself to consider these to have been purely coincidental occurrences.

The talk show interview provides evidence in my own mind that the cream of our society's crop rises to the top in the "celebrity" world. The current plethora of reality shows that abound is providing evidence to me that most people just "don't belong" as having any celebrity status, as evidenced by the lack of aptitude for conversation that these individuals regularly demonstrate whenever they're interviewed on our nation's TV talk shows. The wit of *real* celebrities makes them a joy to watch when they're being interviewed. Whenever a spontaneous exchange of comments is made between the host and his or her guest is when a celebrity interview achieves its greatest potential for audience appeal.

To me, cheerleading is art masquerading as sport. Allow me to unveil what I believe to be the true premise behind cheerleading. I imagine that roughly 100 years ago, there was once a local team of ball players (any type of ball players will do for this hypothetic) who regularly lost to a rival team of local ball players. I conjecture that somewhere amidst the dejection of losing to this rival team, in an attempt to salvage something positive from this all-too-familiar occurrence of losing, one of the gathered male supporters of the losing team noticed that the collective group of females who had come in support of the losing team were more attractive than the opposing team's assembled group of female supporters. I then assume that eventually, at some point during a future contest, a group of these attractive female supporters was eventually paraded out into a more conspicuous area of the contest site, with the false premise of "rallying the troops" being presented as the motivation behind them being positioned thusly. But what the intent of displaying these women actually was, was to make it more readily apparent to the opposition and its respective fan base that, although the losing team's neighborhood may contain an *inferior* pool of genetic material from which to choose to represent their population group in contests, *athletically* speaking, it should now be known and understood by everyone involved that the losing team's neighborhood still contains the *superior* pool of genetic material from which to choose to represent their population group in contests, *aesthetically* speaking. And ever since then, I suspect that schools and towns have been attempting to make that same aesthetic, genetics-inferred statement about their own represented population groups by virtue of their careful attention to what they consider to be "superior female physical traits" during the selection processes of their given school or town's cheerleading squads.

Pragmatic Sexuality

The sexual overtones of that previous hypothesis conveniently enough allow me to now make a smooth segue into the subject matter of this present chapter. I'll now dare to venture into the delicate subject of human sexuality, with my own personal perspective on the male and female relationship being revealed in the process. This will be done at the risk of ruffling some prudish feathers, but done nonetheless, in hopes of stimulating some thoughts or discussion on the subject, and in the end, hopefully reaching some heretofore unrecognized truth or truths in regard to the male/female relationship, which, were they to be realized, could help advance this cause towards a much-needed constructive end.

The unsolvability of the female mindset (as I mentioned earlier in regard to large-scale and quantum physics) also fits in nicely with the "yin-yang" model of existence when compared to the straightforward mindset of the male. When you consider the length of time that men have devoted towards trying to figure out women (thousands of years), and the quality and quantity of inquiry that's been devoted to that subject (billions of intelligent heterosexual men over the course of those thousands of years thinking about the problem extensively throughout the course of each of their respective lives), the amount of research that's been devoted to this subject is staggering. Human brains are great problem-solvers. If any problem were to be presented to the world, in hopes that someone somewhere might eventually discover a solution to it, somebody somewhere likely *would* eventually figure out a solution to it. And it would probably occur a lot sooner rather than later. It only took roughly thousands of men roughly one hundred years to figure out how to split the atom once it was discovered, but man is still relatively baffled by women even after so much greater of an effort has been expended on his collective part towards solving their mystery. It might seem reasonable to assume that testosterone concentrations/levels might account for behavioral/sensibility differences between the sexes, until the presence of the gay and lesbian portion of the population is introduced into the equation. Gay men have high levels of testosterone, yet they have female behavioral characteristics and lesbian women have high levels of estrogen, yet they have male behavioral characteristics. So an alternative cause besides chemical discrepancies has to be considered. I guess it must have something to do with the "wiring" in the brain that creates these behavioral/sensibility differences between the sexes.

Every person has within him or herself a varying degree of capacity for romantic involvement with another person. Whenever a person finds another person who shares the same relative capacity for romance that he or she does, they call that other person a "soul mate." "Soul mating" is an issue of linking together people of similar romantic sensibilities or congruity. But I have trouble seeing any congruity at all between the sexes. Not to sound calloused, but in my experience and observations, it seems men are nothing more than a means to an end for women. Sex is a bargaining chip for them that's to be exchanged for individual physical security, or secure housing, or gifts, or drugs and/or alcohol. Whenever a guy takes a female out to a restaurant or some type of show, that guy seems to simply become a "going out factory/machine" in the eyes of the female. And that seems to be what's appealing to her about the male, not the male himself. It also may be the case that the social status that accompanies "having a man" is of greater significance to a woman than the relationship itself. It's certainly not the physical intimacy that a relationship entails that attracts women to men. They couldn't seem to care less about that aspect of relationships, and the prospect of one of them ever being in a relationship with a man who had a "one track mind" that revolved around sex is probably on their list of worst-case relationship scenarios. On the other hand, as far as the male's perspective on relationships is concerned, the ultimate measure of a man is his woman. Whichever man has the greatest woman is the greatest man. And here's the male criterion for judging female "greatness": to a male, no amount of inner beauty could ever compete with the potential that outer female beauty holds for him in its ability to attract himself to a female. And developing that emotional connection with the female is of the utmost importance to him, because for a man to be in love is for him to know what happiness looks like, tastes like, smells like, sounds like, and feels like. The object of a man's love is the embodiment of fulfillment to each of his given senses. I want women to understand that to a male, sex with a beautiful woman is probably a hundred times more important than anything else in the world; and a woman's beauty is therefore a hundred times more important to a man than any other aspect of her personality or nature. As I mentioned earlier, emotions are so powerful. And romantic feelings are amongst the strongest. That's why to men, our romantic relationships are the most important aspects of our lives, and why the quotation "All's fair in love and war" has been able to withstand the test of time. I suggest that the "difficulty talking to women" that men experience is less a result or manifestation of our anxiety over "not knowing what to say to them" or our fear of possible rejection by them, but more so, rather, a reflection of the potential gravity of the situation that our souls are sensing whenever they're confronted with an opportunity or situation the potential ramifications of which may lead to the greatest overall impact on our collective extended happiness in life.

Sex is a spiritual/transcendental act. And generally speaking, I'm amazed at the female's blasé attitude in regard to it. I think the biggest flaw in men's thinking in regard to figuring out women is his assumption that women share the same sensibilities that men do. I personally have a problem with females who don't like to touch or be touched by a man. Unfortunately, though for me, this group of women may include all of them as far as I know, because I haven't found one who likes to either touch me or be touched by me (my sample group in this regard is admittedly small, though). Although physically consummating a relationship is purported to strengthen it, it's been my experience that the sex act separates the individuals in the relationship and becomes a source of resentment in the female. Perhaps it's the animalistic nature of the act itself that makes it such a turn-off for them (and "yes," I acknowledge the possibility that it could also just be "me" that's the problem. Again, who asked you? Again, just kidding).

Personally, I consider my sex drive to be just about the best part of myself. Why so? Because of desire. A life that's devoid of desire is a wasted life. And because the desire for sex is so much stronger than practically all of the other human desires, it's therefore the desire that provides man with the most meaning to his life. Life is defined by emotion (but on a side note, it isn't always easy to connect emotional responses to specific occurrences or incidents because those responses can be delayed in their onset. A person can be in either a good or bad mood and potentially not even know the reason why). Aside from the gratification of orgasm, lying down with my arms around a woman, allowing for intimate skin contact between the two of us to happen, which promotes the growth of passion within myself, is the greatest of all possible personal experiences for myself.

I propose that general "female aversion to physical intimacy" is a significant, detrimental factor in a large percentage of unhappy and failed marriages in our modern society. Guys are "horny" and women aren't is the problem, basically speaking. I suggest the satisfaction and emotional bonding that physical intimacy is designed to create is failing to be achieved (or at least sustained) in most relationships. We're subjected to a cruel circumstance/reality in which men and women are incompatible to be, figuratively speaking, joined together. The physical parts are compatible but that's usually where the compatibility ends. The comparative romantic ideals/expectations of men vs. those of women seem to be at opposite ends of the emotional spectrum from one another. But at the risk of being labeled an eternal optimist, I'd like to believe that the collective destinies of the sexes aren't doomed to one of perennial incompatibility, even as much as history seems to indicate otherwise. I'm convinced that mutual sexual desire on the parts of males and females can be somehow cultivated. The receptivity of the male to sexual stimulation has never been in question, and it seems, as well, that the physical-sexual sensations of the female can also be easily cultivated, given the right circumstances; which leads me to believe that sexual compatibility between the sexes isn't a lost cause. The female's body parts are still receptive to sexual stimulation, it's just that the emotional barriers that females possess need to somehow be overcome in order for mutual physical-sexual compatibility to be achieved between the two of them.

Why do some women seem to enjoy sex and others don't? The answer may lie in their upbringing. I've deduced a pragmatic solution to this dilemma of emotional-sexual incompatibility between the sexes, albeit an entirely morally unimplementable one. I'll mention it, though, for plausibility/conjecture's sake. Without delving into what the actual, unseemly *specifics* of the methodology might entail, I'll suffice to say that I suspect that due to the profound psychological and emotional effects that childhood sexual abuse has proven to have on the females who've had the ungodly misfortunate of having been subjected to it, and also based on the coinciding "acting out" that I've heard of that later manifests itself amongst these same females who've undergone such abuse, it occurs to me that certain types of childhood sexual abuse that's directed towards females might actually result in said females eventually coming to demonstrate the personality traits and behavioral characteristics that have come to be idealized and embodied by the theoretical paragons of female companionship that are better known as the "Stepford Wives" (a.k.a. perfect wives). But I digress from this morally bankrupt suggestion in favor of continuing to direct our discussion towards a more morally solvent one.

Here's only a *slightly* less monstrous suggestion as a solution to the problem of romantic incompatibility between the sexes, and one that many people might consider to have been more appropriately suggested during the Dark Ages, but one that I'll suggest nonetheless. The premise is to take a romantically dissatisfied couple and "force" the consenting adult female partner into engaging in physical sexual relations with her male counterpart until she "learns to love it" (even as antiquated and barbaric of a notion as that may sound to be). Any couple that struggles with the concept of physical intimacy within their relationship would basically begin engaging in "rape therapy," albeit a consensual and sensual form of it. This form of therapy would capitalize on the antiquated concept that biology can overwhelm emotion, as the female's body would theoretically become more and more receptive to sexual stimulation as a result of her continued exposure to it, and as a result, her emotional inhibitions would consequently diminish as they would eventually be supplanted by her own physical desires. But is this concept considered to be antiquated due to its proven ineffectiveness or because the methodology would be viewed contemporarily as being socially repulsive? I believe volunteers and scientific investigation would be needed in order to adequately answer such a question. But I'm afraid volunteers could never actually be obtained for such experimentation due to the fact that practically every female who isn't currently engaging in regular intimate relations with her partner would likely believe any increase on her own part in her own level of "intimacy output" within the relationship would likely only result in herself experiencing a direct decrease in her own level of satisfaction within that relationship, and that she would therefore likely never agree to participation in such an experiment in the first place. Such females would likely just as soon get divorced than agree to participate in such "nonsense." Upon having now suggested such a methodology of treatment, though, I can't help but wonder if the seemingly outlandish, or perhaps even *offensive*, nature of this suggestion in the eyes of the reading public might well inspire this book to become more commonly referred to as "The Rape Therapy Book;" which wouldn't be at all bothersome to me if it were ever revealed to be that this type of methodology were actually proven to be a worthwhile form of treatment for couples.

And to further outrage (or at least leave further aghast) the reader, I would also seriously suggest the application of physical restraints to the female's limbs during certain aspects of such therapy sessions. Escapable restraints would be preferable to inescapable ones due to my belief that a futility of limb movement needn't be the object of such restraints, rather merely, the occupation of the limbs from engaging in movement at that time, as I believe the female's receptivity to stimulation is enhanced when her role is reduced to that of one of passivity in the sexual dynamic between herself and the male. I believe sexual gratification is enhanced when there's only one active partner at a time, and that it's conversely reduced when both partners attempt to fulfill active roles at the same time. Don't be too quick to poo-poo any of these suggestions, though. I don't see anyone else solving the American marriage crisis. Do you?

Along these same lines of stimulation and arousal, I suspect there's a range of body fat percentage that can be contained within the female that can prove itself to increase the female's receptivity or sensitivity to experiencing sensual or sexual pleasure. Look at the definition of "voluptuous." Although it's become synonymous with a woman being "full-figured," Webster's defines it as "full of, producing, or fond of sensual pleasures." When a woman contains more body fat, she's better able to sustain a pregnancy. Wouldn't it only seem natural then if there were to exist a direct relationship between a woman's level of sensual receptivity and her body's conduciveness to pregnancy (since, of course, an increase in the frequency of sexual activity results in an increased possibility of achieving pregnancy)? Of course it would.

At certain ages and sizes, women are sexual objects to men. This is the case in spite of our culture's attempts to steer the male sentiment towards a less superficial ideal. And also, in spite of our society's mores that speak to the contrary, the sexual attractiveness of the female blossoms at puberty, which occurs long before the age of eighteen. So, when any society directs indignities towards any man who finds a teenage girl attractive, such a practice seems misguided to me.

How coincidental is it that both a woman's beauty and her fertility seem to decline at the same time? Is it possible that there's some sort of "youth maintaining" agent that's produced within the female body amongst its cocktail of menstrual hormones? If such a chemical were to exist, and if it could then be synthesized, it could then theoretically be pharmacologically prescribed to women to aid them in their battle against aging. But "battle" seems like a bit too strong of a word to use in this regard, though, for I find the aplomb with which women seem to handle the time constraint with which they are all faced in life in regard to their beauty and fertility, very impressive. To me, it seems like women don't even seem to notice the clock ticking away on them, a circumstance that works to our society's benefit I believe. Because I'd hate to imagine how men would react to being placed in a similar circumstance. I don't believe women hit the "panic button" nearly to the extent or force to which men theoretically would be doing so in this regard were their roles reversed. Doesn't it seem ironic, or at least odd, that a young female can be the source of greatest attraction to a male, while an older female by contrast can be the source of greatest aversion/repulsion to that same male?

The concept of providing females with breast implants is problematic on two fronts. First, since they're artificial, they render that area of the body as a nonerogenous zone for the female. Secondly, implants don't look or respond like human tissue to the male, so many males are unable to become aroused by them. The viscosity/thickness of breast tissue (as evidenced by the amount and percentage of mammary gland tissue contained within the breast vs. the amount and percentage of fat tissue that's also contained within the breast) must be within certain ranges in order for the ability of manual manipulation of the breast on the part of the male to produce gratification within the female; and those self-same ranges must also be maintained within the breast in order for the male to achieve maximum gratification from his own manipulation of said tissue. It's a completely reflexive relationship, and therefore, one in which I think humans were clearly designed to engage. Just at the manual manipulation, or kneading, of bread dough results in the activation of the living yeast within that dough, and then culminates with the rising of that dough as a result of that process, the kneading of breast tissue, as well, results in the "coming alive" of that tissue, which culminates with an increase in lactation production and responsiveness/receptivity on the female's part to that tissue's manipulation. I also want to believe that if or when a female achieves an optimal ratio of specific tissue types within the breast, she, at that time, achieves a higher level of divinity than a common female. This is evidenced by the effect that the attainment of this optimal ratio has on the male soul whenever the male happens to encounter such a ratio within a female (you can call it the "gawking" factor, humorously speaking). And as I stated earlier as a belief of mine, anything that speaks to the soul is divine. But this supposed fact, were it to actually be true, in regard to this "divinity-achieving-potential" of the female body, will, for whatever reason, always elude the female intellect. Just as children will never realize that their own innocence makes them divine, either.

With all due respect to women, I also believe that they're, as a gender, woefully ignorant in regard to the general male sentiment towards the breasts themselves. My own informal interaction with males throughout the course of my own lifetime leads me to suggest that a conservative estimate of about 1 out of 50, or a more liberal estimate of about 1 out of 100, males are actually "breast men"; with the remaining 98 percent -99 percent of the remaining male heterosexual portion of the population being practically totally unconcerned with women's breast sizes. Sexually and relationship-wise, it's a nonissue for the overwhelming majority of men. Every man says that he *likes* large breasts, but only "breast men" feel it's *important*. "Breast men" can be spotted from a mile away because, if you're a male and you ever happen to talk with one, the conversation will inevitably lead towards that subject.

Should the apparent rift between men and women be determined to stem from a cultural maladaptation between the sexes, then what I believe would be another worthwhile study to undertake in regard to human sexuality would be to first gather "female situational receptivity characteristics or responses to physical intimacy" (more commonly known as female "turn-ons"/ "turn-offs") amongst wives of differing world cultures, and then, compare those responses with both that wife and her husband's own respective reported levels of sexual satisfaction that they each report to be experiencing within their marriage. Upon analyzing the data, it could then likely be determined whether or not a relationship exists between certain female turn-ons/turn-offs and successful marriages. And if such relationships *were* determined to exist, then whatever female turn-ons/turn-offs were determined to be compatible with successful marriages could then perhaps begin to be implemented or incorporated into the lifestyles of failing marriage population groups, in hopes of eventually achieving success within them. Forgive me, though, if I don't hold the *Playboy*'s *Playmate* "turn-ons/turn-offs" responses to be scientifically reliable enough data to accept as evidence towards possible conclusions that might be drawn towards this end.

The offerings at bars and restaurants in regards to food, drinks, prices, and atmosphere are all relatively the same all across America. The only significant variable that separates them all is the relative attractiveness of each bar or restaurant's respective employee base. As I suggest that if it isn't already one, it should become an institutional practice amongst the single male population of this country to make employee attractiveness a primary factor in its collective decision-making process as it relates to which bars or restaurants to frequent. Atmospherically, in my opinion, gay bars are superior to straight bars due to their lack of a "hostile vibe" and because gays go there just to "have fun."

Pragmatic Discourse

Whenever an argument happens to occur between two individuals, it's been my experience that each person immediately arms him or herself with a shield or cloak of dismissiveness regarding the other person's point of view, and the combatants almost always refuse to acknowledge even the slightest possibility of validity regarding the other person's arguments. It would be easy for anyone in such a situation to get the impression that his or her arguments were being completely ignored by his or her opponent and that the other person "hasn't heard a single word that he or she has said." Although "winning" an argument may never be an acknowledgment that's ever conceded to in such a situation, it's at least possible to get the satisfaction of knowing that your points have at least been *understood* by your opponent if people would begin to make it a point to request that the other party paraphrase their arguments back to them at some point during their "discussions."

Anyone who displays a dismissive attitude towards others' opinions is demonstrating ignorance, just as anyone who acts certain that his or her own opinions are correct is also demonstrating his or her own ignorance. Definitiveness on anyone's part generally leaves a bad taste in my mouth whenever I happen to encounter it, and I'm finding it to become more and more an affront to my sensibilities the older I get. Nobody knows anything for sure, generally speaking. The use of sound reasoning doesn't even necessarily portend the arrival at correct conclusions. One of the smartest things that a person can do is to consider the possibility that every theory to which he or she has either ever ascribed or has even ever been exposed to may turn out to be 100 percent wrong. Certainty is the hallmark of fanaticism. Confidence that isn't accompanied by experience is a sign of danger. Unless you've experienced something, you don't know. In fact, I'd likely attribute any inaccuracies that are contained in this very book as occurring as a direct result of my own lack of experience in whatever subject I happen to be covering at the time. It should likely come as no surprise to anyone that I probably don't have as much to say on these subjects as other authors do. I don't have much of a varied work experience, I lack relationship experience, I don't have any children, I haven't done much coaching or teaching, I haven't had a lot of obstacles or hardships to overcome in life, I received a formulaic education, and I've never been the object of persecution or discrimination. I've had about as unremarkable and "incident-free" an existence as a person can have up until this point (thank God). So, it may probably seem ironic that someone with as little experience as myself would be touting the virtues of experience, but that's the way I see things. Two of the most valuable pieces of human knowledge that experience can provide are the knowledge of the general range of human capabilities and the knowledge of general human tendencies. Knowing what is or isn't normal enables a person to correctly surmise or determine the correct response that's required for any given situation. The gospel is a testimony to the value of experience. Jesus, as both the presumed savior and judge of humanity had to become human and experience life as a human in order to earn those rights/entitlements. Speaking of experience, is it me, or is it difficult to have feelings about something without there being a physical experience attached to it? Maybe that's the reason why I've never cared about any of the tragedies that I've ever heard about that have ever happened out there in the world, such as 9/11, natural disasters, school shootings, etc. You name it, I don't care about it. But then again, maybe I'm just a monster.

Although I claim to vilify "dismissive" attitudes, I'm not suggesting that people shouldn't be dismissive towards taking other people's advice, though. There's a good reason why people are dismissive towards taking others' advice. Again, I believe that the reason speaks to the nature of our souls. Our souls tell us what aspects of life are or should be important to us. Giving advice is insulting to an individual because it's the same as telling that person that his or her conscience is incapable of providing trustworthy guidance, or that perhaps his or her brain is incapable of correctly interpreting his or her soul's messages and desires.

Recounts of past experiences have no redeeming value. That's why story-telling is considered the lowest form of conversation. Generally speaking, the past needn't be brought up because it serves no practical purpose. I place "complaining about something and never doing anything about it" in the same category. In an ideal world, any person who would be identified as the type of person who tells the exact same stories over and over again would be prohibited from telling those stories. Discussion/debate is the highest form of conversation because discussion leads to revelation. And revelation leads to revolution. And revolution leads to regime change. This is why discussion isn't embraced in our modern church construct. The church leaders know that their roles, and therefore, their salaries, are unwarranted, and they, therefore, don't want their religious populace to find or figure this out. So, this is why they continue their stranglehold on the conversation with their weekly, brainwashing monologues that they call sermons.

Discussion, like writing, is also a refining process, but it's superior to writing because it involves a multiplicity of minds. One mind could never produce the depth of knowledge that a multiplicity of minds could ever produce, because every mind by itself is only prone to a certain range of thought. But every mind is different from every other mind and can think in ways that no other mind can. When you combine minds in a discussion group, the output is exponential. This is because every mind is feeding on and feeding back on the information that's produced by every other mind. Just as one mind produces and edits information in the writing process, multiple minds produce and edit information in the discussion process. Discussion cultivates growth of perspective and the development of new ideas.

Possibly the best thing about phone "texting" is that is prevents people from cutting each other off when they're talking to each other. You'll always get to complete your thoughts whenever you text. Plus, it provides proof of what a person has said. Also, it's impossible to yell at the other person with whom your texting; which is usually a good thing.

Pragmatic Politics

It seems to me that the political arena would necessarily be the only satisfactory lodging place for anyone who's truly philosophical in nature, as there are potentially limitless possibilities for the application of philosophical beliefs in this field. Philosophy is in essence a search for the best way to solve problems, or at least, control contingencies. These contingencies can range from dealing with natural and man-made disasters, to dealing with our society's desire for improvements in our living and working conditions, to controlling people's behavior. I suspect that one of the main reasons why the hairs on all of the leaders of the world's heads always turns white is because it only takes at minimum *one* resourceful person from *anywhere* in the world to potentially wreak havoc on any of their given societies. Political leaders would like to be able to account for this contingency, but they've all been as yet up to this point in history, *unsuccessful* at doing so. Basically, if all of a society's members ever felt completely safe all of the time and were always completely satisfied with every aspect of their lives, then the need for politics would cease to exist.

The mechanism of politics is simple: if the leaders who create policies that affect a community make wise legislative decisions regarding that community's future, then that community will prosper. By contrast, if these same leaders make ill-advised decisions regarding that community's future, then that community will eventually languish. It's the useful application of the mechanics of politics that's so difficult to achieve. Traditionally in politics, poor decisions are a result of two distinct scenarios: (1) in good faith, a community's leader makes legislative decisions that he or she feels are in the best interest of his or her constituency, but that leader unfortunately fails to accurately forecast the impact of those policies, and the community winds up suffering as a result of those ill-conceived policies. (2) In a betrayal of his or her constituency's trust, a community's leader places his or her own financial interests ahead of the interests of his or her constituency, and as a result, implements policies whose goals are aimed simply at the achievement of that politician's own reelection. Either way, the community's economy ends up in a tailspin. When skillfully practiced, political office is a difficult position to hold, due to the tremendous foresight that's required of its practitioners to accurately anticipate the ripple effects of policy implementation.

In my opinion, the ideal president would have had every job there is before taking office. But because that's implausible, I believe the president should have advisors appointed from every line of work, no matter how many hundreds of advisors that might entail. This is again because experience is the only way to truly know a subject, and it's therefore the best defense against getting "snow jobbed" in regard to any issue.

Allowing private citizens and companies to contribute money to the campaign funds of political candidates is one of the most ill-conceived notions of all time. No wonder we're still driving gasoline powered cars when the oil companies can contribute billions of dollars to help finance political campaigns. Not to mention the obvious price-fixing that oil companies are engaged in, as evidenced by the ability of British Petroleum (BP) to easily compensate practically any and all lawsuit claims with which they were presented in the southeastern U.S. in regards to that company's oil spill in the Gulf of Mexico in 2010. Look at the annual profits that are publicly reported by these companies every year. There's no competition-based reduction in pricing taking place. Here's a sneaky question that could be posed to every political representative in our country: "We know that *you're* not corrupt, but at what point in their political careers do you suspect that the *other* politicians become corrupt?" Their answers would probably be very revealing.

The jury system is also an ill-conceived institution. The accumulated loss of productivity that's sustained through the act of extricating the jury pool from their jobs during the week, combined with the tax payer burden of having to pay all of the jury pool members for their services every week, make it an expensive undertaking. The money could be considered well spent if their verdicts were just, but look at the results. They don't know what they're doing. The jury pool doesn't understand the law and doesn't want to be there. Elect three judges, people who both understand the law and are interested in the justice system, to try all of the cases, with the majority ruling prevailing. Provide the judges with 24-hour security and place their families in "witness relocation" programs if necessary to maintain the integrity of the office. If the judges still end up being corrupt, find out how they were "reached," eliminate that method from becoming an option in the future, elect three more judges to throw the corrupt ones in jail, and start the process over again from the beginning.

Doesn't it seem likely that we've had the technology for a while now in this country to have enabled us to transition our nation's military force into becoming a remote, mechanically-based one, rather than still maintaining the ancient, antiquated model of a direct, human intervention-based one? I wouldn't be surprised if there were some sort of voting-related conspiracy at the root of this delay in this transition.

But political inadequacies or inequalities such as the ones I've been mentioning obviously don't bother me much because I don't try to do anything about them. Nonpoliticians, such as talk-radio hosts, who are impassioned and feel compelled to share their insights on the political affairs of the day, make an open betrayal of their own consciences with every successive salient comment that they make in regard to each political issue, because anyone who claims to both care about his or her society and who also has a solution to some political shortcoming that's been instituted by that society should feel compelled to actually *do* something in response to said shortcoming rather than feeling contented to simply *gripe* about it. People who speak with certainty on political issues should either run for office or stop complaining. They should become a force for change. President Truman was onto something. The problem with politics is that everyone passes the buck. People make the mistaken assumption of believing that there's a separation between the implementation of political change and their own actions. Solutions are everyone's personal responsibility to create. Only when "nonstop talking" becomes vilified and "personal action" becomes the only acceptable response for citizens to make will improvements in our society begin to occur.

Negative predictions about our society's future come at a cost to the audience of such predictions. Such predictions have a detrimental effect on a person's peace of mind; which would be permissible should a prediction prove to be accurate, but I suggest that such predictions be considered criminal if not so. Since our nation's inception, there's been no shortage of predictions regarding its imminent demise, but none have ever come to fruition.

Anyone to whom casting a vote is the extent of his or her contribution to the political process is a joke of a person to me. Any concerned citizen should aim the scope of his or her political influence to be broader than merely casting a relatively meaningless vote.

Abortion is, of course, a volatile issue. But I suggest that a much more significant tragedy than "aborted babies" is the death of, let's say, a thirty-year-old human who has had all of those years of effort and expense spent on him or her before any return on that investment can be made.

On the topic of social reform, I have a couple of thoughts. As I've been saying, I don't think anyone knows what something is like until they've experienced it. So, because I'm not old or underprivileged, I don't know if our country has a justifiable ethical imperative to subsidize our nation's elderly and our nation's welfare recipients. I don't know if these programs' recipients have a legitimate ethical claim to taxpayer money or if they're just being selfish and greedy. On the other hand, I *do* believe anyone who's served our country's military in order to preserve our freedom likely deserves whatever means of support this country has to offer him or her until he or she dies. But do all old people, in general, deserve money that they haven't earned, just so they can be kept alive at our nation's expense? I don't know. Likewise, do welfare recipients who are capable of working deserve this self-same entitlement? I don't know the answer to that, either. Here are some alternative suggestions, though: people who haven't come up with a way to live outside of government support could be given aptitude tests and offered commensurately appropriate jobs to perform in order to support themselves. Alternative lifestyle choices might also be able to be offered to these individuals such as subsistence farming, or a return to the concept of debtor's (type) prisons (but with hopefully better living conditions contained within them than their predecessors). I guess I'll have to wait until I'm either old and/or get on welfare to decide whether or not I feel that I'm genuinely entitled to all of the government handouts that are out there for this segment of the population or not. This is of course assuming that such programs will even continue to exist in future times. It would seem typical of most people's luck, of course, if these programs were to become defunct just as one of us were about to be able to start taking advantage of them, right?

The concept of "welfare reversal" is an idea of mine, the possible implementation of which is to be considered by anyone who believes that putting our country's needs above the individual's is the proper stance for someone to take in this country. Here's the premise: what do you think would happen to our country's economy if all of our welfare recipients were given whatever jobs they wanted? Let's say that the "unemployable" would be both replaced and trained by the "employable." The "employable" would then be on welfare and it could then be assumed that they would have an easier time getting off welfare due to their possession of employable skill sets. And the welfare burden would therefore, presumably, become greatly reduced whenever these now currently unemployed people began eventually and gradually rejoining the workforce, as would be expected of them to do.

Pragmatic Engineering

Uncoordinated traffic lights are and have been a bane of commuting for the entirety of our society's exposure to them. One conspiracy theory that would make a lot of sense to me were it to ever be exposed to be true would be if the car and tire manufacturing and oil company lobbyists were involved in our lifelong exposure to uncoordinated traffic light systems. Cars and tires wear out faster and use more gasoline because of them. It's ridiculous to suggest that in this day and age that the technology doesn't exist to keep traffic flow moving more expeditiously. On a side note, I've found getting away with speeding and running stop signs and red lights to be a very gratifying experience, as I'm sure everyone else who has also done so will also attest to. And couldn't you just kiss any of our fellow drivers out there who are thoughtful enough to flash their lights at us in an effort to alert us to upcoming cop cars that are positioned to give us speeding tickets? These people are the greatest.

Telling people to "drive carefully" is a hollow sentiment, as are the daily radio traffic reports. People are going to drive in every given situation the way their experience and instincts tell them to drive, and no differently, regardless of any advice to do otherwise that they may receive from "friendly neighbors." The only time anyone is listening to radio traffic reports is when they're already in their car and en route to their destinations. So, bequests on the parts of traffic reporters for commuters to "give themselves more time" are therefore rendered moot. The only useful traffic report these reporters could provide is to inform the listening public of which commuters are "screwed" and which ones aren't. Speaking of cars, the frame design in stock cars these days is ridiculously ugly. Why don't they just make the cars look like Lamborghinis? The manufacturers would make some sales *then* and wouldn't need a bailout.

Restrooms are wonderful inventions when it comes to providing humans with comfort during their bowel movements, but I much prefer urinating out in nature as compared to using a restroom, any time. Such a convenience would also reduce the frequency of required bathroom cleaning on our parts. It's too bad that it's illegal to do so, though. I wish there were legal "pee partitions" in grassy areas that we could be encouraged to use if we ever felt so inclined to do so. Can you tell that I'm running out of topics to discuss, yet?

Pragmatic Application

Although this entire book has basically revolved around the premise of applying knowledge, I still somehow feel as if I've thus far managed to avoid delivering any actual "nuts and bolts" plans for the application of any of the so-called knowledge that I've provided here. And if that were allowed to continue, I'd have to conclude that I would have failed in my mission to completely live up to the pragmatic ideal that I've been working so hard to promote here. So, this chapter is where that deficiency is hopefully quelled.

I'll now explain what I'd specifically do with my life if I were to ever have the good fortune of being able to do with it just as I pleased. Humans thrive and survive on hope. Hopelessness is as fatal a disease as any. At the time of my writing this, I haven't yet given up my hope of finding and maintaining a romantic relationship with a female, as I am now and have always been without satisfactory companionship. Neither have I given up my hope of somehow obtaining enough money to invest in the type of lifestyle that I'd like to someday enjoy,; as I am now and have always been without sufficient capital to do so (not that I'm complaining about either of these circumstances, mind you, it's just that I could foresee them potentially becoming the death of me at some point). The former hope is more important to me than the latter, but this chapter will focus on the latter.

I'm serious about wanting to get people involved in some sort of regular, philosophically-oriented discussion group. And to me, a poker game is the ideal format and forum for the implementation of such a construct. I don't believe poker has as of yet realized its greatest potential for utility within our society. Sure, it's a fun and popular game to play, but I believe there's also a separate, untapped vein of utility "lurking" inside of it just waiting to be discovered. Allow me to expound:

(1.)   Poker is a simple game. Let's say that it takes roughly 40 hours for the average person to become both familiar and comfortable with the game's rules and procedures. And let's also say that it similarly takes roughly the same amount of time for him or her to develop a reasonable sense of strategy to employ towards its effective game-play. Now, once this designated level of comfort and execution is achieved by an individual, the learning curve for him or her at that point regarding the game becomes much more plateaued. And upon arriving at this plateau, as far as playing the game is concerned, little attention is then required on his or her part in order to make correct decisions regarding his or her own strategic initiatives. This fact allows for an experienced player to be able to divide his or her attention even while still being actively engaged in a hand, without any coinciding reduction in his or her decision-making capability regarding that hand; which then enables him or her to both listen to and engage in discussion while still playing.

(2.) Then there's the overwhelming presence of "downtime" that occurs within the game for practically every player involved. This occurs as a result of all of the folding of hands that occurs throughout the course of any given "deal" or "hand" and, by extension, throughout the course of any given poker session. And once a player folds, there's nothing more then for him or her to do for the remainder of that hand. So, as a result, all the players who've folded their cards during a hand are then completely free to engage in discussion with one another. And because decision-making usually takes such little focus on the parts of the remaining players in a hand, there's no need for the bystanders to become overly concerned about disrupting these players' decision-making processes by means of their banter, because, as was just explained, these remaining players don't require their attention to be undivided in order for them to be able to effectively play out their hands.

(3.) Next, there's the common scenario of long hours of play associated with the game, and the fact that the traditional seating arrangement of the poker table is coincidentally and conveniently enough conducive to the engagement in conversation amongst the poker game's population group. There's basically "no limit" (no pun intended) to the amount, degree, depth, extent, and variety of conversation that could theoretically occur amongst such a group of players during and throughout the course of any given poker session. All of this opportunity for conversation could also become more easily facilitated were it to also be made known to everyone involved that "conversation" was to take the precedence over game-play during their group's encounters, and that this stipulation should come to be regarded as the norm. With such a focus in mind, I believe that within a relatively short amount of time, a civil, organized model of conversation could easily become cultivated within and amongst the participants of such a gathering.

(4.)   There's no need to actually involve gambling in this poker construct, either, especially since it would be likely be illegal to do so. Players could simply be provided with a designated, limited amount of chips with which to work on a daily basis and work out from there. The fact that there would only be a finite amount of chips available for each player to use would hopefully induce said players towards playing the same brand of poker that "real money at stake" poker players would play, as the decisions that any of these "fake money at stake" players would make would be contingent upon the relative sizes of their respective chip stacks, just as would be the case if "real money" were to actually be involved (but to me, without getting too much into poker theory, such a concern regarding individuals' styles of play shouldn't even enter into the minds of any poker players, because good players simply make adjustments and allowances for *any* potential styles of play with which they might come into contact, and then make the most logical possible game-play decisions for themselves based on their interpretations of whatever particular styles they're confronted with). To further promote the concept of "meaningful stakes," players could keep running totals of their daily chip amounts, and perhaps the "big winner" for the year could be awarded some worthwhile prize.

I believe the above-suggested methodology could serve as a good general model for developing an effective discussion group, but I'll now explain the specific management style and modifications to this model that I'd personally employ were I to ever undertake such an endeavor. First, I like the idea of having a facility with 24-hour access to it, with everyone involved being both a key holder and a manager of the facility, so that people could therefore play at their own convenience and, as a result of myself having placed such a large amount of trust in them, would also hopefully feel compelled to take responsibility for the facility's maintenance, as well. Secondly, because I believe in Christianity, I'd like for the facility to ideally become a "modern church alternative." On Sundays, I'd like to present the opportunity for everyone involved to have a Memorial Supper there, where any interested believer could "eat the body" and "drink the blood" of Jesus as part of the Bible-mandated memorial service that was designated to be held by Christians in his honor every week (as I understand it). Secondly, I'd like for religion to be an especially encouraged topic of discussion amongst the poker players whenever they play; politics being encouraged to be discussed extensively, as well, as I believe these two topics would most likely provide the most potential fodder for discussion amongst any available topics, and are also perhaps the two most potentially influential topics towards helping someone find direction in his or her own life. As far as the religious conversation is concerned, I'd encourage any and all agnostics, atheists, and believers alike to willingly, openly, and unapologetically, "put their two cents in" towards any particular points of contention that might arise, as varying viewpoints make for well-rounded discourse. But I wouldn't be surprised if alcohol might need to be at least an initial offering at the facility in order to help attract newcomers to both the location and the concept.

Eventually, if this premise became popular enough, and if enough money could ever be procured (not that I believe that profit should ever become a goal whenever Christianity is involved), other "fun-based" activities for participants could also become offered as well, such as indoor gymnasiums for playing basketball and tennis, weight rooms, swimming pools, music and art rooms, and the like. All based solely upon the initial premise of promoting discussion. Maybe even a school could eventually be founded, with pragmatic tenets being placed at the center of its educational philosophy. But I'd be happy for now to simply settle for a free poker game that I enjoyed being a part of. But I have to now admit that this suggested model of recreational offerings isn't an entirely original concept on my part, though. Even within my own hometown, previously owned recreational facilities have been purchased by local churches and converted into the same type of recreational facilities that I've just suggested. Which, aside from my own personal disagreement with these churches regarding their ideologies and methodologies, I'm very pleased to see, as they're obviously offering the same exact activities that I believe in and that I would offer, too, were I ever presented with the opportunity to do so. The ultimate symbols of success for me in regard to any conversational poker program to which I might ever become a part would be if all of the Christians involved were to eventually become a group able to provide for itself a new, more powerful meaning to the word "church," and if *all* parties involved with the program, Christian or otherwise, were to deem themselves lucky to live in the town in which they did as a direct result of their involvement and experience with the program itself.

These have been all of the opinions that I have to share for now. Thanks for your indulgence.